T0354669

Down
the
Road

LINDA E. RENNELL

iUniverse

DOWN THE ROAD

iUniverse books may be ordered through booksellers or by contacting:

iUniverse
1663 Liberty Drive
Bloomington, IN 47403
www.iuniverse.com
844-349-9409

ISBN: 978-1-6632-3313-4 (sc)
ISBN: 978-1-6632-3474-2 (hc)
ISBN: 978-1-6632-3312-7 (e)

Library of Congress Control Number: 2022900639

Print information available on the last page.

iUniverse rev. date: 06/24/2022

Dedicated to
my husband, Kenny;
my son Eric and his wife Karen
and their children Drew, Jack, and Molly;
and to my daughter Monica,
her children Emma and Cameron,
and their father Jason

PREFACE

This memoir has a little something for everybody. It is part autobiography, part biography, part love story, part small business guide, and part life-changing event. These snapshots of our lives—my husband Kenny and me—embody our lives together. I hope that as you share my journey, you will reflect upon your own life and find a more than nugget or two of happiness there.

The title of this book—***Down The Road***—defines our life's path. There were always roads to choose in our life together. We seldom took the direct road, in most cases traveling side roads along the way. The chapter titles are places where Kenny and I lived at different times. When we talked about our goals, he always said, "Let's do that down the road." Ultimately, for every challenge we met, our motto *"down the road"* took on a whole new meaning and significance.

I'm a motivated dreamer. My life partner helped me pursue and achieve these goals. Together we found the guts to persevere against all odds.

Won't you take a trip down my memory lane? Let's go ***Down The Road*** together!

CONTENTS

CHAPTER ONE

Somerville/Elm

- - - - - - - - - - - - -

"Puppy love" is defined as a short-lived, adolescent crush. Kenny and I redefined the term and gave it whole new meaning. Our lasting relationship proves that resilience pays off, time and time again!

I was born Linda Emma Celli on December 30, 1952, in Cambridge, Massachusetts, and grew up in Somerville, Massachusetts. Somerville was a big city, mostly hard-working, blue-collar families of Irish and Italian origin. People took public transportation, walked, and rode bikes; shopped and attended social gatherings. The streets, lined with sidewalks on both sides, were clustered with two- and three-family dwellings on tiny lots. Essentials and penny candy filled the corner stores. The street trees were either very mature, with roots that buckled the asphalt, or new, twig-like saplings, wired to tall sticks for support. Parking was limited, and often we placed barrels or chairs in parking spaces to reserve them for friends and family with automobiles. Although crime was common in other neighborhoods in the city, ours was secluded from drugs and theft, a blessed oasis. We went about our business in our little circle, mostly unaware of what went on elsewhere in the city. Sometimes ignorance is bliss.

Our modest, first-floor, five-room apartment was across from a playground known as Conway Park. Since my back yard was a blanket of hot-top, the park with its grass and swing sets was my recreation spot. Our Somerville Avenue home had an outdated parlor, a kitchen with printed wallpaper, two small bedrooms, and a small bathroom with wall-to-wall pink-and-black tile. A bar room dominated our neighborhood, so nights were noisy from drunks shouting obscenities as they were thrown out into the street.

| My parents, Mary & John Celli | My Aunt Lorraine and Uncle Bob Gallant |

My mother, Mary, was a little heavy-set, but very attractive with curly brown hair. My father, John, was about five-foot-nine-inches tall, with a medium build and wavy brown hair. They met while dancing at an Italian club.

My brother, Johnny, six years my junior, was a husky boy who loved all kinds of sports. As a boy, he played Little League baseball, with Uncle Bob as his coach. I went to most of his games and learned to keep score. Johnny was a good athlete, and he helped me become knowledgeable about baseball. He also liked basketball. I often shot hoops with him and his friends. (To this day I can still rack up the points.) Once he got to high school, football was his sport. Although he was the apple of my mother's eye, I loved being his big sister.

My maternal grandmother, Nana Emma, lived with her daughter, my Aunt Lorraine, and her husband, my Uncle Bob. Auntie and Uncle had no children. Nana Emma had lost her husband in his early forties from complications with blood clots. Auntie had vowed never to leave her mother alone, so the three of them lived together on the second floor.

Auntie was petite with straight brown hair. She worked in the city clerk's office at Somerville City Hall. Uncle Bob was short, very handsome, and masculine. My brother and I reaped the benefits of having an extended family close by.

My paternal grandparents, Catherine and Joseph Celli, were both of Italian descent and came from North Cambridge, Massachusetts. They had four children: three boys and a girl. My father, John, was third in line. His older brothers were Joseph and Frank, and his sister was Dottie. John was easy-going and family-oriented. His mother, to whom he was very close, passed away before his marriage to my mother. After Catherine died, the Celli family tried to stick together, but because siblings do not always see eye to eye, John and his brothers and sister went their separate ways, each with different values and goals.

My maternal grandparents, Emma (Nana Emma, born in Italy) and Joseph Guaraldi (born in Brazil) married in Italy at ages fifteen and nineteen, respectively. Joseph, a tall slender man with olive skin and dark wavy hair, came first to America with his brother seeking work. Emma and her sister-in-law traveled by boat to America, landing at Ellis Island. Their husbands waited on the shore for them. Emma and Joe settled in Sagamore, Massachusetts, where Emma easily made friends. She was hard-working, cooking, cleaning, and doing laundry to keep the house in order.

Emma was naturally pretty, light-complected, of medium height, with flawless skin and crimped light-brown hair. She loved playing cards with her friends on Friday nights.

Eventually, Emma and Joe moved to Elm Street in Somerville. She delivered both daughters, Mary and Lorraine, in the apartment's living room, never spending a day in the hospital. In a few years they had saved enough to buy a neighborhood grocery store on Somerville Avenue. The family lived above the store. They worked hard and made a good living because their local customers were loyal and paid them well.

My maternal grandparents
Emma & Joe Guaraldi

My mother Mary and her sister Lorraine were two years apart, very different in personality and temperament. Mom was high-strung and confrontational. My aunt was quiet, nervous, and more of a peacemaker. My grandmother was somewhere in between. With that mix, there was always lots of drama among the women of the house.

In contrast, the men were cool and got along great. My dad always defended my uncle (his brother-in-law) and was as protective of him as a big brother. My uncle, raised in Maine, later moved to Chelsea, Massachusetts. He went from living in the woods to where the action was in the city. Uncle could be feisty when he drank, but my dad always remained calm. One night after a few too many drinks, Uncle Bob got into a fist fight with a neighbor on the sidewalk over a parking space. Dad broke it up and took Uncle inside to sober him up with black coffee. Since no one else in our family liked to drink or party, it was not always easy for my uncle to conform to this conservative lifestyle.

Down the road, Uncle Bob settled down and made his wife Lorraine, her happiness, and their marriage his top priorities.

CHAPTER TWO

Elm/Porter

Kenneth Joseph Rennell was born March 31, 1952, in Boston, Massachusetts. His family first lived in a four-room apartment in Cambridge, Massachusetts. Kenny's dad, Joe, was a tall, handsome man with a husky build, of French descent. He worked on tall skyscrapers in Boston, employed as an ironworker. His mother, Rita, of Italian heritage, was petite, with light-brown hair. Joe and Rita met over their love of dancing, the same way my parents met.

Kenny's paternal grandparents were French Canadians, both of whom died at an early age. His dad, Joe, was the youngest of six, so he was raised by his five older sisters. (In contrast, his son Kenny became the oldest of six and helped raise his five younger sisters!) Two of Joe's sisters had children out of wedlock but kept their maiden name, so Joe, Kenny, and Kenny's son Eric were the only ones to carry on the Rennell name legitimately.

Kenny's maternal grandparents, Nana (Mary) and Pop (Richard) Volpicelli, owned a three-family house with rental garages on Elm Street in Somerville. Nana was gray-haired and under five feet tall. She was dedicated to her three children, Esther, Richard and Rita (Kenny's mother), and was happy when they were all together. I loved Nana's spunk and independence. She secretly obtained her driver's license, but never sat in the driver's seat.

Pop was fair-skinned, short, bald, and blue-eyed. He walked and took public transportation to his various jobs and enjoyed socializing with his many friends in the North End.

Nana and Pop Volpicelli lived on the third floor of the Elm Street house. Nana and Pop's daughter, Esther, husband Paul Strati, and children, Paul, Jr, and Dianne lived on the second floor. Their son, Richard Volpicelli, his wife, Rita, and their children Dickie, Eileen, Kathy, Michael, and Joanne lived on the first floor. When Richard and family moved to Lexington, Kenny's family, the Rennells, rented the first-floor apartment and moved in from the small, four-room apartment in Cambridge that they had been living in.

Nana's two daughters lived under the same roof. Like my own mother and her sister, Kenny's mother Rita and Aunt Esther were total opposites. Esther worked full-time and was motherly, whereas Rita stayed home but was less nurturing.

The Elm Street home had white clapboards and black shutters. It was a welcoming home base for family gatherings and holidays. Kenny, his parents, and his four sisters—Linda, Paula, Claudia and Marsha, all younger—were grateful for the larger living space. Yes, he was the only boy! The girls shared one room, and the pantry became Kenny's bedroom. He was happy for the privacy, but he had to slouch when he got out of bed to avoid hitting his head against the slanted ceiling.

Kenny appreciated having relatives living upstairs, no matter the family dynamics. Aunt Esther and Uncle Paul knew that Kenny's family struggled financially, so they always took him on vacation with them. Kenny and his cousin Paul, only a year apart, became best friends, like brothers. They spent a lot of time together. They made lots of wonderful memories at New Hampshire attractions and elsewhere.

In the late 1950s, when I was in third grade, my parents, along with my aunt and uncle, purchased a two-family house on Porter Street near the Somerville Hospital. The mint-green, vinyl-sided house had front and back porches and a backyard. I was thrilled to have grass and now I could plant flowers. We lived on the first floor and Auntie and Uncle lived on the second.

As it turned out, Kenny and I were now neighbors, although we did not know each other yet. My street—Porter—and Kenny's—Elm—were perpendicular to each other. Our house was at the top of the hill and his was at the bottom.

With the move, I switched from Carr Elementary to Morse Elementary School. Luckily, I was a social child and made friends quickly in school and in the neighborhood. Although Marianne and Barbara became my new friends, I missed my Carr school friends, Joanne—my first friend—and Ann, who was in first and second grades with me. Ann's family also moved to another part of the city, but we met again in high school, and we've been friends for more than fifty years since. Joanne and I reconnected many years later and reestablished our early friendship, too.

My brother Johnny and I loved living downstairs from family. Uncle Bob was a truck driver for Grossmans, a local lumber and hardware chain of stores. When things went on sale or were damaged, he got them at a discount for us. We were amazed and grateful when he brought us a swing set and a three-foot-deep round swimming pool. I always had a special bond with my Aunt Lorraine, whom I often called LaLa. She took me shopping, to the movies, and to the bakery. We were a lot alike: we both had easy-going personalities and loved new clothes and shoes. My parents purchased my back-to-school clothes, and my grandmother and aunt bought enough outfits so I could wear a new one each day for the first week of school.

Nana Emma was usually at home and I often went upstairs to watch her cook or iron clothes. She would tell me about her youth as a girl on the family farm in Northern Italy. Her mother died when she was only ten years old, so she helped care for her dad and younger siblings. She spoke mostly Italian and filled in with the English words that she knew. This way, I learned to understand the language but not speak it.

We saw each other on Sundays at Saint Anthony's Church, an old, two-level, Italian building, at the 8:30 a.m. High Mass with the organist and choir. It was held on the upper floor. The first floor was dark and dingy and smelled of lit candles. Elderly parishioners attended the early Mass every weekday.

We never talked to each other then, because of the nuns in full black-and-white habits who sat at the end of the pews like guards. We sat in strategically arranged seats, robotically sitting, kneeling, and standing on cue throughout the Mass, never understanding a word of the sing-song Latin it was conducted in.

Both of us being Catholic, Saint Anthony was our patron saint and came to have great significance to us throughout our lives. It turns out that we each received First Communion and Confirmation at the same time, although we didn't really meet until after that.

Kenny and I came from two different worlds. I was sheltered, lacked independence, and had strict parents. Kenny was street-smart, took care of his sisters, and was self-sufficient. Despite our different family lives, however, we both were kind, respectful, and considerate.

I came to know Kenny after I made friends with his next-door neighbor Debbie. He came around while we sat out on her porch. Sometimes a group of us walked home together from church or school, so we often talked as we went along.

Kenny had a genuine smile and a nice personality. Right away my instincts told me he was a good person. He was a leader, not a follower. I loved his confidence and determination. He spoke his mind and never wavered about how he felt about anything. In contrast, my family considered it disrespectful to speak one's mind, so I rarely had the courage to do the same.

Secretly, I wanted to be like that! I was always ambitious and had dreams, but kept them to myself. After my first day of school in kindergarten, at four years old, I remember telling Mom I wanted to grow up to be a teacher and a principal. She reminded me grimly that no one in our family had ever gone to college, not even a boy. "Don't you want to get married and have kids?" she would say. When I responded that I wanted to do both—go to college and have a family—she snickered at me. I never had Mom's support about my goals.

On the other hand, Dad was always in my corner and he believed in me. He made me believe that I could do whatever I wanted in life. He seldom voiced his opinion or corrected Mom's comments, but behind closed doors, he always told me how proud he was of me and gave me encouragement. He was so gentle and kind, and when I was with him, he always made me feel calm and safe. My dad and I would sit on the couch and watch TV. He loved wrestling, boxing, roller derby, and other contact sports, an interesting contrast in an otherwise docile man. We also enjoyed talking about his work and my school. I loved how easy our conversations were. He would hum or whistle "You are my Sunshine." It made me feel so special and loved.

Mom stayed at home while my dad worked. This was typical back then. I always had clean clothes, good food, and a spotless home. I remember coming home to the aroma of Mom's cooking and baking. From upstairs came the sound of the old Singer sewing machine pounding stitches from thread to bobbin. Nana Emma and Auntie made clothes from patterns and I was always in awe of their talent. My material needs were always met, but my emotional needs? Eh, not so much.

When Johnny and I were young, our parents would go out dancing with family and friends on Saturday nights. They went to either the Dante Club or the Progressive Club. Nana Emma would babysit us and we'd watch The Lawrence Welk show. I loved the music! After hearing Myron Floren play polkas on his accordion, I begged my parents to let me take accordion lessons. Luckily my dad's cousin taught lessons in North Cambridge and got me a discounted accordion. I practiced daily and won a few trophies at local competitions. Sad to say, I lost interest as a teenager and do not remember how to play.

My family looked fine from the outside, but inside there was lots of yelling and turbulence, arguing and disagreements. Mom was very high-strung and intimidating, and her nervous condition caused havoc in our home.

Kenny's family was much different. They were boisterous, inside and out. His father was similar to my dad, kind and easy-going, but when provoked by his mother, he would explode. This caused a lot of drama in his large family, too.

Kenny started his work career as a delivery boy for a grocery store, working before and after school. At twelve, he began working for the *Somerville Journal*, a weekly newspaper. On Thursday mornings at 4 a.m., his boss would pick him up and they'd drive to Waltham where the paper was published. Kenny would sort and wrap the papers according to regions for the delivery boys. Then he'd go home, have breakfast, and go to school. While other kids played sports after school, Kenny went back to work from three to six. He would have liked to play hockey or basketball, but it was not an option for him. Even at that age, he was saving money to buy his first car. He was always passionate about cars—model cars, old cars, and new cars. He was not the best academic student and hated homework, but he knew everything about cars and engines. He was much happier in a garage than in a classroom.

Kenny was tall, dark, and thin, with brown eyes. I was short with dark, curly hair and brown eyes. Other than those brown eyes, we could not have looked more different. There was a one-foot difference in height, so I always wore heels or wedge shoes to look taller.

I always thought it was quite a coincidence that my maiden name was Celli and Kenny's mother's maiden name was Volpicelli. In fact, my mother went to Somerville High School with Kenny's uncle, and his mother graduated with my aunt.

Elementary School Class Photos
Linda Celli and Kenny Rennell

Now that Kenny and I lived in the same neighborhood, we soon discovered that we had a number of friends in common. We all rode bikes and skateboarded, and played hopscotch and dodgeball. When I went to Southern Junior High, Kenny was still at Saint Anthony's until eighth grade. When he transferred to Southern for ninth grade, we finally had classes together.

The middle school was a nice two-story building near Union Square. A select group of students who had done well in elementary school were chosen to take advanced classes, called College Prep. Luckily, I was one of them. Our College Prep group learned modern math, studied Shakespeare, and took language classes.

This is where I met one of my best friends, Maria. She was very social with a great personality. She excelled in French and I in Math, so we helped each other study. We both came from Italian backgrounds, were hard workers, and enjoyed each other's company. Maria was a loyal, caring friend and I am happy to say she is still an important part of my life today. We have been through many good and bad times together. Her husband,

Frank and Kenny were friends; our sons played sports together; and our daughters danced at the same studio.

My other friend, Ann, from Carr Elementary, reconnected with me in high school. We picked up where we left off in second grade, as if no time had passed. She was always kind and considerate and we were good friends. Later, at Boston State, we both were Elementary Education majors and took most of the same classes.

By the time I was fourteen and Kenny was fifteen, we traveled in the same social circle. On Sunday nights, a group of us all went to the CYO socials together. We roller-skated and danced, then went for pizza. Some of my girl friends liked Kenny and I would fix them up with him, but it never worked out. I liked a few other guys, too, but again, there was no chemistry there.

Anne, me, and Maria   1956 Chevy

Soon, Kenny began to walk me home after the dances. My dad met him and liked him. Before I knew it, Kenny was dropping me. He'd sit on the front steps and we'd talk. Little by little, I noticed that he was cute, a nice boy whom I was finding attractive. My friends told me he liked me as a girlfriend. One summer afternoon, as my dad and I sat on the back porch, I told him that Kenny had asked if we might date. True to form, my dad was on board with me.

That was a big year for Kenny. He had finally saved up enough money to buy his dream car—a 1956 Chevy Bel Air. It was a shiny turquoise blue. He didn't even have his permit yet. He was only fifteen years old, but he was achieving his dreams. His grandmother let him keep his Chevy in one of her garages. I was so proud of him! I was one of the first people he showed it to, and I was so happy for him. We hugged each other. The instant chemistry made sparks fly! I was really falling for this guy whom I had always thought of as just a friend. One day when I was sixteen, I sat on my front steps waiting for him, and he came running up the hill, bursting with pride, waving his driver's permit in hand!

He bought a hood scoop for the car and we spent hours together in his garage installing it. We laughed and talked and had loads of fun. He taught me the names of the tools, then called me his assistant, which thrilled me.

One day he invited me to go to the Somerville Theater on Sunday to see "Beach Blanket Bingo," one of the beach-party films popular in the 1960s, starring Frankie Avalon and Annette Funicello. I begged Dad to talk Mom to give me permission and he did. He always advocated for us. Mom listened to him. They trusted my judgement, because I had consistently made good choices.

Our first date was on August 17, 1967. Dad later said that he could see that Kenny was a good kid who had his head on straight. Dad's endorsement made me like him even more. I could not believe it: I had my first boyfriend!

Some of our field trips were to New Hampshire to ski. I was just learning, so I stayed on the bunny slope, but Kenny was an excellent skier. On the way home from a field trip to Byfield, Kenny and I kissed for the first time. I was smitten. A few weeks later he asked me to go steady, and I enthusiastically accepted. I went home and thought about him all night. It didn't matter than I never slept a wink. Now he would call me a few times a week. We were together all the time, so everyone knew we were an item.

In September, CYO began again at the church. We had Sunday night socials and field trips, and meetings and dances were held in the basement of the school hall. We became friends with so many nice people from our parish. At the dances, when the disc jockey put on a slow song, Kenny would stroll over to me and grab my hand, and we'd slow-dance together. His arms around me felt so amazing and I hated when the song ended. I was always a romantic and still am!

I was so happy, but our mothers did not approve. They thought we were too young. We both were determined to be together, so we did what we had to see each other and sneaked around and lied so we could meet up. We were so comfortable with each other, I realized this could be much more than "puppy love."

By this time I was at Somerville High and he was at North Cambridge Catholic. Some pressured us to date other people, but we refused. Once Kenny had his driver's license and registered his car, we had more freedom to date. We spent a great summer going to the beach, drive-in movies, and mini-golf.

A young priest, Father Joe, chaperoned our CYO events and mentored all of us. Lots of us became couples on these trips, but Kenny and I were one of the few pairs that endured. After the bus dropped us off at the church, we would walk home, hand-in-hand, stopping first at Craigie Park and make out on the bench there. At first this was awkward, but then I began to enjoy the kissing and the hugging. I really liked him!

My very first job was working in a laundry when I was fourteen, but it wasn't long before I found a better part-time job at Bradlees department store, which I consider my first real job. I liked to buy clothes, which I could get at Bradlees, and by that time I was saving towards college. With my growing relationship with Kenny, I was thrilled to work in the store's Automotive Department. I learned about spark plugs and mag wheels, which gave me more things in common with him.

Kenny was still working at the *Somerville Journal*. We spent some money on dates, but more often we watched television at my house or worked on his Chevy. How he loved cars! He applied all kinds of knowledge into his passion, much of it from car magazines he subscribed to. We joked about who was first in his life—his car or me. This was always debatable!

Our junior year in high school was difficult since we were at two different schools. Even though our mothers disapproved, our fathers were always in our corner, as were our friends and most of our family members. Dickie started dating Linda, who fixed up Paul with Carol. It was cool that Dickie and Paul were first cousins, as were Linda and Carol. The six of us went out a lot together. I was the only non-related one but we were all friends.

Kenny and I took each other to our junior prom events. I was so excited to get all dressed up for him. He was most handsome in his tuxedo. I wore a long, peach-colored gown with a white coat, and he gave me a rose corsage. We doubled with friends and had a great time at both events. We took his Chevy to his prom and decorated it with streamers. That night he said he loved me and wanted to marry me. Those were the most exciting words I had ever heard!

Instead of a prom, Somerville High held a music concert with dancing in the auditorium. We went in casual dress, danced all night, and had a grand time. He was my guy and I was his girl.

Auntie Lorraine, Uncle Bob, and Nana Emma saw all of Kenny's good qualities and were happy for us. Kenny was head-strong about what he wanted in his life and I was grateful that he included me in his plan. I was quiet and easy-going, but when I saw something I wanted, I went for it. I definitely wanted a life with Kenny. We complemented each other. My strengths balanced his weaknesses and vice versa. So, we plowed forward, working hard at school and work. Love was in the air and I was so happy despite our obstacles.

Dad worked full-time at Raytheon in Quincy on an assembly line. He had a second job at a cold-cut store. One day he came home from the deli not feeling well. His chest hurt. Back then one's primary care doctor—a general practitioner—handled everything. My parents never sought out specialists, so my dad was never referred to a cardiologist. Stents and bi-passes were never discussed as options. He never received a second opinion. All I remember is Mom telling me that he had angina, and that when he felt chest pain, he put a nitroglycerin pill for under his tongue. This was the first of his three heart attacks.

The poor man was always fatigued and pale. He couldn't go back to work. He became depressed and lost his sense of purpose. Back then, a man was defined by his work ethic. Dad's disability forced Mom into the workplace. She was not mentally or physically ready for this and she let everyone know it. It was hell for everyone.

Mom found work as a lunch lady at a local elementary school. She never got her license, so my father began to drive her everywhere—to her work and for errands and shopping. Being her escort helped to renew his self-esteem.

I worried day and night about my father's health, full of anxiety and fear of losing him. Most nights I could not fall asleep worrying if he was okay. I would wake in a panic, having dreamed that he had died. My dad was my safety net and my security, so I did not want to imagine my life without him. The thought of that haunted me.

It was at this time that Kenny found out his mother was pregnant again. This would make six children for them, and he worried about how they could afford another mouth to feed. There would be eight of them crammed into his grandmother's five-room apartment. Kenny helped them as much as he could, but he had a lot on his plate, too.

His parents were on a bowling league on Sunday nights so we babysat his sisters. They were all so cute and he loved them all very much. We played with them and he made them giggle. The oldest, Linda, was quiet and kept to herself. Then came the little blondie, Paula, who always was happy and kind. Claudia was next, spunky and strong-willed. Marsha was a toddler, and Maria was a baby. I'd change her diapers and feed her. After we tucked them all into bed, we would watch TV and chat.

The Celli Family   The Rennell Family sisters

I was determined to go to college to become a teacher. I asked my guidance counselor if he had applications for a local college that was inexpensive and that I could get to with public transportation. He handed me an application for Boston State College and I made my plans. I had to take the SAT's and pray I got in. I did. My test results were decent and I was accepted. Then, in order to raise the tuition, I worked full-time in the summers and part-time during the school year, saving as much as I could. The college held no open houses or class visits, so I never saw the campus until I stood in line to register for classes.

By now, all of our schoolmates had "steadies," the girls receiving friendship rings from their boys. I hoped for one too, but I doubted that Kenny could afford one. Most of my friends' boyfriends were older. with more spending cash than Kenny. Somehow, he scrounged up the money, though, and bought one. At first his mother wouldn't let him give it to me. In her mind, we were too young to go steady. Maybe that was true, but Kenny fought back, and he presented me with the gorgeous, blue sapphire birthstone ring a few months later. I was thrilled! Once it was on my finger, no way was it ever coming off. We were committed to each other. I have it still, in its original blue velvet box in my jewelry box.

Things got rougher for our families. Dad's second heart attack put him back in Somerville Hospital. About this time, Kenny's mother gave birth to his sister, Maria, born with Down syndrome. Having a special-needs child was difficult enough, but little Maria was sickly as well and spent a lot of time at Boston Children's Hospital. Despite that, she was a sweet, precious little girl.

One night in early summer of 1969, Kenny called me and we went out. He was nervous and quiet. His parents had bought a house in Tewksbury, he said, and they were moving at the end of August.

My heart shattered right then and there. Tewksbury? Where the hell was that? Way up north, twenty-six miles away. It might as well have been on the other side of the country.

Even though Kenny had a car – his '56 Chevy Bel Air – he was only allowed to drive it locally, and only in good weather. If we were to meet, he'd have to borrow his dad's car, and only if it was available. We commiserated, but then reassured each other that we'd figure it out, the way we always did. This was our biggest challenge yet!

The poor guy, his entire school life had been in parochial school; now he'd be entering his senior year at Tewksbury High, a public school. Neither of us was happy about it.

At the end of August, the Rennell family moved to Tewksbury into a big four-bedroom house in the middle of the woods, on a dead-end street with lots of land. They had homing pigeons, chickens, ducks, and a goat. Kenny finally had his own room and his own space for himself. He came to love the suburbs, but it was a huge change from urban Somerville. And of course, it was so far away from me. A call from a pay-phone cost fifty-five cents for a measly three minutes. Too expensive! And so were long-distance charges from our home phones. To keep our relationship strong, we wrote letters to each other. I loved writing; Kenny did not. But he surprised me with his dedication to it. I still treasure those innocent and sincere love letters.

I was alone in Somerville without Kenny, with a sick father and a difficult mother, trying to find a way to afford to go college. I loved my father and Kenny so much, but now it felt like I might lose them both. Our house was in constant emotional chaos. There was no other way to put it: That summer of '69 sucked!

I had so looked forward to an amazing senior year, but it was anxiety-ridden instead. With Kenny at Tewksbury High School while I was still at Somerville High, we were worlds apart. He used his dad's car on the weekends when his dad let him and if he had gas money. Another requirement we hadn't counted on was that he couldn't borrow the car unless he brought along one of his sisters, Linda or Paula.

Paula was fine. We always had a blast with her, joking around, and she was happy to spend some time alone with her brother on the rides coming and going. They were very close.

On the other hand, Linda would sulk in the back seat with Chippa, Kenny's dog, bored, and never say a word. After an hour, she'd beg him to take her home.

Then Mom found out about our threesome dates, and insisted that we include Johnny, too. It was more than annoying, but we did what we had to do to spend time together.

Maintaining a long-distance relationship was a struggle, with our busy schedules and our financial stress. Our only salvation was that Kenny's Nana and Pop still lived around the corner from us in Somerville. When he could borrow the car, Kenny drove down and stayed with them. They liked him and approved of our relationship, so they often covered for us.

Kenny and Linda at York Beach, Maine

I had left Bradlees for a new job in Davis Square at Cummings Clothing Store. My shifts were on Thursday and Friday nights and all day on Saturdays, so I could study during the week. I spent weeknights filling out college applications. Although I was busy, my heart ached so much and I missed Kenny.

Everyone knew we were a couple but after he moved to Tewksbury people doubted that it would last. Many guys said they would date me if Kenny and I fell apart. That was flattering, but it did not turn my head in the least. I wanted no one else but Kenny.

Some of Kenny's new friends tried to set him up with other girls, too, but he refused. We were both determined to make our complicated relationship work.

Kenny called or came down as often as he could, but it was never as often as we wanted. In between times, I was lonesome and disappointed. The separation led to a lot of argument and it felt like we were falling apart. At senior prom time, I took Kenny to mine, and my dad let him drive his new Chevy Impala. The theme was "Cherish." We surely cherished and loved each other, but doubts arose between us and I began questioning, "Is this enough?"

21

The day after the prom we went to Hampton Beach with our friends. Other couples held hands and frolicked in the waves, while we rushed through our picnic lunch. Kenny checked his watch every few minutes. He had to leave early to go to work at a gas station on Main Street in Tewksbury, worried that he'd run into bad traffic on the way home and be late. It pissed me off that he had not taken the day off so we could have a nice romantic time together. There was no romance in our air that day. It was a disaster.

We used to be so in sync with each other, but now we were distant and growing apart. Our chemistry had changed and we began to annoy each other. We both knew it but we did not know how to change it back to what we used to be. As the song says, "We were losing that loving feeling."

I wanted to go to his prom, but he said he wasn't going. He acted weird when I asked him about it. I found out later that he did go, when I saw a picture at his house of him with another girl, all dressed in prom clothes, and I was crushed. This was the first time he had lied to me. Could I trust him anymore?

Situations at both the Celli and Rennell homes continued to be strained. Both houses were very hectic and demanding. Our families relied on each of us to help out in many aspects. Kenny babysat and helped his family financially as he could. At this time Kenny's father, working in construction, didn't always have a job in bad weather. Kenny had five sisters and a mother who could not work. At my house I drove when my father couldn't, helped manage my brother, and did errands. My brother was almost a teenager and didn't do well in school, so I helped him study and tried to guide him away from the wrong crowd.

One day we were visiting Kenny's Uncle Dick in Lexington, talking about plans for the future. He knew Kenny was mechanically talented and great with engines. He suggested that Kenny attend East Coast Aero Technical School at Hanscom Airforce Base in Bedford, Massachusetts. The two-year associate's program awarded a degree as an aircraft mechanic. The program was half-academics and half-shop, ideal for Kenny.

When Kenny told his family about a higher education, they flipped out. They counted on him to continue helping to support the family by working. Our relationship was a threat to them and their financial status. They didn't understand a couple of things. One was that graduating with a degree as an aircraft mechanic meant opportunities for Kenny to get good-paying jobs, and this could be beneficial to them. The other was that once people reached adulthood, they usually got married and started their own families, which didn't automatically mean abandonment of their parents and siblings.

Despite the family objections, Kenny looked into the aviation school. He respected and admired his Uncle Dick and took his advice. Uncle Dick got Kenny an application, and he applied. Tuition was a concern, but Kenny figured that he could cover that with his jobs. He went for an interview and got accepted. Lots of students had part-time jobs on base, so he applied as a janitor. To pay for school and expenses, he kept his gas station job and worked seasonally at an ice-cream shop.

At the time the state schools were the best for the education major I was aiming for. I was thrilled to be accepted to Boston State, a four-year commitment, along with lots of my friends. Other friends enrolled at Salem State College. Either way, I was thankful to have friends share this new venture with me. I was finally going to be a college freshman.

Except for my dad, no one in my house was happy about my going to college, either. The pressure to raise money for tuition weighed heavy on me. My aunt, uncle, and grandmother said they would help me as needed for books, lab fees, and other college expenses. I was excited but nervous. If my home life had been more stable at this time, I would have felt more confident than I did. But I encouraged myself by reminding myself that after I graduated from college, Kenny and I would be free to marry.

We were both totally overwhelmed by everything that was going on. Pressure from our families made us both feel guilty. Were we being selfish and disappointing our families? For the first time, we were indecisive.

One night when we were out on a date, Kenny said we needed to talk about something. I was curious but scared. He was confused. He had begun to second-guess himself and question his decision to go to East Coast Aerotech. He thought we should forget about school and get married right away instead. This was so out of character for him: he was always determined and confident in his decisions.

It was thrilling to know that he loved me so much to want to marry me right then, but I insisted that it was too soon, not the right time. Although I was afraid to lose him, I felt strongly that we should stick to our original plan. We had shown ourselves to be responsible, mature and ambitious, and I didn't want to jeopardize that.

I loved him and wanted to marry him but I knew we were too young, at ages seventeen and eighteen. I told him I really wanted to be a teacher. If I didn't pursue this career, I might regret it or resent him in the future, and I didn't want that to happen. I asked him if he was asking this to run away from the problems at home, and pointed out that we couldn't afford to live together yet. Besides that, my parents would certainly never approve, so we would have to elope. What he asked meant bigger changes to our plans than we could handle.

He grumbled that he might enlist in the Air Force instead. But I was afraid that if he did that and something ever happened to him—the Viet Nam war was still in full swing—that I would regret that. We were at an impasse and it tore us apart. Before he left—pissed off at me—I begged him not to be hasty and to take his time to think about everything.

That night I prayed that I made the right choice. Nothing mattered if Kenny was not with me. I wanted him in my life, but like he always said, that had to be down the road.

We were apart for a few tough weeks, during which Kenny's cousins and friends encouraged him to stick to his original plan to go to the aerotech school. Then I asked a friend drive me up to Tewksbury to see him.

He and I went for a long ride, and he let me know he had changed his mind and would go to East Coast. Was that a relief to hear!

I hoped he was doing this for himself, not just for me, and I believe he was. He stood strong and realized that furthering our educations was our best option for a successful life together. He promised to buy me a hope chest the next year as a pre-engagement gift. We were stronger than ever, on our way down the road together.

Little by little, after Kenny and I both graduated from high school in June 1970, both families began to accept that we would not be dissuaded from our commitment to each other.

Kenny and Linda
High School Class Photos

One night that summer, while I waited on my front porch for Kenny to arrive, he pulled up in a new blue (his favorite color) Plymouth Duster, a gorgeous sports car with loud exhausts. That was so Kenny. The royal-blue beauty rumbled when he put the key in the ignition.

I had no idea where the money came from to buy it. But I did know is that now, with his own wheels, he could visit more often. My heart swelled with love.

He leaped out of the car. He got his father to co-sign for him and bought it. This car was one reason we would stay together, aiming for our Happily-Ever-After. I knew then that we would be okay. We were determined to make our dreams come true, and even though we were apart most of the time, we were working as a team to do it. We fit together like two puzzle pieces!

In September we both were working day and night, as well as starting classes at our schools. Whenever the stress became too much, I would look down at my friendship ring. It motivated me to keep going. We were always so happy when we were able to get together. Kenny's cousin Paul Strati was going to Boston State, too, as a biology major, and he and I became good friends. He supported Kenny and me without question. He was such a great guy and friend!

In February 1971 we picked out a hope chest on Canal Street right across from the old Boston Garden. It was Mediterranean style and our first piece of furniture together. We were on our way! Most of my friends were already engaged but our day would come. All we had to do was be patient. Down the road, we would get our Happily-Ever-After.

We both studied and worked hard. Our Sunday night dates were more work than play: we spent them studying at the Tufts Library. We laughed, studied and sneaked kisses in between. He stayed with his grandparents on the weekends whenever he could. His Nana, still living down the hill from me, helped him a lot and took good care of him. When he left on Sunday nights to go back to Tewksbury, we never knew just when he'd be back. We managed to see each other once or twice a week. Knowing that was a light at the end of our tunnel.

LaLa and Uncle Bob had a summer home in York, Maine. Sometimes they would take me with them for the weekend. It was only a short walk down a dirt road to Long Sands Beach and the ocean. My grandmother, Nana Emma, often came, too. While Uncle Bob and I went to the beach with the neighbors, she and Auntie cleaned and cooked. They seldom had fun; they stayed indoors most of the time because they didn't like the sand and bugs.

I loved hanging out with my uncle. We always laughed and had fun together. In his small motor boat, he drove quickly over the waves and I tanned myself on the bow. When we stopped to fish, the slow gentle rolling waves made my stomach queasy, so I preferred to fish from the shore. Uncle Bob taught me how to split earthworms to use for bait.

I wanted Kenny to come up for an overnight stay but his parents wouldn't let him. He'd have to sleep on the couch, and Auntie and Uncle were there as chaperones, but that wasn't good enough, I guess. One time, Kenny's cousins Paul Strati and Dickie Volpicelli were taking their girlfriends to Cape Cod for the weekend. Kenny hatched a plot to drive to the Cape with them, make a collect call to his parents so they knew he was there, then drive all the way north to York Beach to be with me. As usual, Auntie and Uncle covered for us. We rode bikes, took long walks on the beach, and went out in the boat. We had pulled off Kenny's trick and all was good.

Or so we thought. When I got home on Sunday, Paul called to report that a bee stung Dickie on Saturday and he had an allergic reaction to it, so they went home early. There was no way to warn Kenny, so when he got home, his parents knew all about Dickie. Caught in a lie, he was grounded for two weeks. Even so, he sneaked down to Somerville a few times. My parents never found out about his grounding, and his parents never found out about our meet-ups.

Kenny graduated from East Coast Aero Technical School in the spring of 1972. A few months before graduation, he was required to take his aircraft mechanic's license certification test. He had been working so much at his three jobs that he had no time to study, so he failed. He couldn't graduate with his class until he passed it. The test and certification were expensive, too - $500 - which he did not have. His parents didn't have that kind of money. I mentioned it to my aunt and uncle, and—incredibly!— they lent him the money, proving their confidence in him. Thanks to them, he completed the program, passed the test, and became a licensed aircraft mechanic. Within a year, Kenny paid Auntie and Uncle back in full.

His first job offer as an aircraft mechanic was in the Philippines. But I had two more years of college and Kenny didn't want to be so far away. He declined the position and looked for employment closer to home. Soon he landed a job as a welder in Billerica while he waited for something better to come along.

For years, my dad tried in vain to get work with the Polaroid Corporation. They finally called him for an interview after he suffered two of his heart attacks. He had Kenny go for the interview in his place, because he knew he would never pass the physical. Kenny aced the interview and was hired to run the battery machine for the instant film with the intention. Kenny viewed this as an opportunity to climb the ladder into a worthier position. It was a steady job, making decent money. Now he could pay his bills, help his family and save for our future.

Around this time, his sister Maria, the youngest, with Down syndrome, was diagnosed with leukemia. His parents stayed at the hospital in town with her when they could, which left Kenny to cook, clean house, and care for his other sisters, besides working full-time. It was rough on everyone.

Boston State was just down the street from the hospital on Longwood Avenue, so I'd visit Maria after my classes. The poor little thing suffering so much! She had to have spinal taps and chemotherapy. It was too much for her body and she passed away in 1972.

Everyone was devastated! I thank God I was there for Kenny. Maria had been like a daughter to him – he was eighteen years older – and he took her death hard. No parents should have to bury their child. It was rough for everyone and all of us – Kenny's parents and sisters, the Rennell cousins, my family, close friends and neighbors – grieved deeply, each in his own way. Little by little, we resumed our lives but we were all melancholy. Seeking happiness again was a challenge.

Kenny had previously asked my father for my hand in marriage. My father gave him his blessing, and when the dust settled after Maria's loss,

28

he took Kenny to his jeweler friend in Inman Square in Cambridge. Those two, my favorite men, picked out my diamond, which made it even more special to me. Kenny put down a deposit and paid for it on a layaway plan, meeting his payment faithfully every month. On September 8, 1972, at Mystic Lake in Medford, he proposed and gave me my beautiful diamond. It was almost one carat. I treasured it then and I still do to this day.

On the way back to my house, we stopped by to visit our friends, Debbie and Al, in Woburn to share our great news. Then we went to Somerville to my house to show my family the ring.

Finally, our parents accepted our relationship. My parents invited Kenny's whole family and a couple of my close friends over for a little engagement party. That night we were so happy and were so optimistic for our future together. With perseverance, we had finally done it and everyone was happy for us. I loved being his fiancée. It didn't take me long to refer to him as my future husband. I couldn't wait to be Mrs. Kenneth Rennell!

Our engagement
(Kenny pointing to my ring!)

Our friends, Maria and Frank DiTucci married in October of 1972, and Dickie and Linda Volpicelli married the following August. I was one of Maria's bridesmaids and Kenny served as an usher for Dickie. Our cousins' nuptials meant we were next! "Down the road" got closer all the time.

My dad's health continued to fail. I worried about him constantly. Whenever I got home from school, I prayed that he was okay, as he was alone in the house most of the day, with Johnny in school and Mom was working part-time as a lunch monitor. I always feared that I'd be the one who came home to find him dead. He was always tired and out of breath.

When I came in, he'd be asleep on the couch. I would quietly check that he was still breathing. Then I'd sit there with him and when he heard me, he would wake up and chat about my day at college and our wedding plans. I had taken up smoking socially at college, so sometimes we would share one while we sat alone. I didn't care—it was his only vice! After sneaking him a cigarette, we'd share a cup of tea. It was our special time together.

Despite these tensions, we enjoyed the Christmas holidays. Kenny gave me a beautiful rabbit-fur coat. I was in shock at his new-found extravagance—furs and jewelry! His first gift to me was an Avon lipstick in a little case, which I saved in my hope chest. Now with money in his pockets, his gifts became more grand.

After the turn to the New Year of 1973, we started talking about wedding dates and venues. Our favorite season was spring, when everything is in bloom and in anticipation of beautiful, sunny days ahead. I've always liked even numbers, so we decided on marrying in 1974 and chose the month of June. We wanted to get married on a Sunday afternoon, better for us because hall rentals were cheaper on Sundays.

In the seventies there were few affordable options for low- to middle-class families on a budget. The upper middle-class booked their receptions at the popular Montvale Plaza in Stoneham. For families in our income bracket, the Steven James House in Cambridge was the place to be. It was nicely appointed and the package deals included catering and flowers along with the hall rental. After Kenny and I and my parents toured the place, we all agreed that this was the place. It was such a desirable venue that no Sunday dates were available in June. It couldn't be in May; that would crowd my graduation. But April 28, 1974, was open. This date was all even numbers, so that made me happy. We tentatively booked the reception hall and Saint Anthony's Church and confirmed that our young CYO priest friend, Father Joe, would officiate at the wedding.

The next weekend Kenny and I talked about where to go on our honeymoon. We decided to reserve the Honeymoon Haven with its heart-shaped tubs and beds in The Poconos in Pennsylvania. Kenny sent away for pamphlets and the place looked amazing. Now we had to save for that.

Kenny was working full-time at Polaroid and had good insurance benefits. He had already worked his way up to the Maintenance Department. He constantly worked overtime throughout the week as well as Saturdays.

My parents were generously paying for the wedding. To ease our need to furnish our first apartment, my grandmother offered to buy us a bedroom set. Then Kenny's parents offered to buy a kitchen set. Finally, my aunt and uncle offered to help purchase whatever else we would need. That left Kenny and me to get a living room set. We went to the wholesale furniture store on Canal Street in Boston, where he had bought my hope chest, and put a red velvet couch and arm chair on layaway. Our goal was to pre-pay for all of our furniture and honeymoon, so whatever monies we received at our wedding could be put toward the down-payment on a house. Kenny tried to pay for everything so I could finish school. I contributed whenever I could. I paid my tuition in full each semester, so I didn't have student-loan worries.

All of these sudden wedding plans threw my school plans off kilter. I had promised Dad that I would graduate before I got married and I wanted to honor that promise. I went to my college advisor, who listened to my dilemma: I had to finish school earlier than I had planned. She recommended summer school in 1973, which would set me up to meet my student-teaching requirement in January of 1974. Theoretically I would be complete my academics in December of 1973 and could shoot for a substitute-teacher position in a local Somerville school in the spring. I would graduate and receive my diploma officially in the middle of May 1974. That would meet my obligation to my dad.

Then I worried that if I doubled up on schooling during the summer, I couldn't work full-time, to raise tuition for my final year. Auntie, Uncle, and Nana Emma came to my rescue once again, promising to help me financially as I needed. Thank God! We were off and running!

Dad was getting worse. He was always short of breath and rarely felt well. I worried about him all the time. On March 1, 1973, a Thursday, he and I had a quick dinner of French toast together. I was on my way out the door to my part-time job, and neither my mother nor my brother was home that evening. Dad left to join his bowling league. I usually got home about 9:30 p.m., and he usually came in around 10:00 p.m. That evening after I got home, Mom, Johnny, and I sat in the living room watching the Dean Martin Variety Show. About 10:20 the doorbell rang. It was our neighbor, Jerry, who also bowled with my father. He said that my father had collapsed while bowling and was rushed by ambulance to Somerville Hospital. He said it didn't look good. We all immediately got dressed, including my grandmother, and Jerry drove us to the hospital.

When we got to the emergency room, a doctor came out and reported that Dad had expired from a massive heart attack. (To this day whenever I hear the word "expire," I cringe.) We couldn't believe it. He was only forty-seven years old.

Mom asked if we could see him. I didn't want to, but I did. The idea terrified me. Johnny stayed with my grandmother while Mom and I went in. When I saw Dad with my own eyes, lying so still and pale, reality set in. This was the worst night of my life. The world would never be the same. Death robbed Dad not only of his life but also of my future and of Johnny's future. It was not fair!

My aunt and uncle were in Las Vegas at the time, vacationing with friends of the family, who happened to own the local funeral parlor. They all flew home immediately to help us plan the wake and funeral. The funeral directors were very helpful and kind to us. We were all overwhelmed. Mom was beside herself. Poor Johnny was only fourteen. I was twenty, a junior in college, almost an independent adult, but I still relied heavily on Dad's wisdom.

How would we get through life without him? He did not deserve to be gone at such a young age. He would never walk me down the aisle at my wedding and give my hand to Kenny. He would never see me become a teacher. He would never meet his grandchildren or great-grandchildren.

Thank God through this entire nightmare I had Kenny to comfort me when I cried, and boy, did I cry a lot. My Uncle Bob stepped up as a father figure for both Johnny and me. He had loved my father. They weren't just brothers-in-law, they were best friends. Uncle and I had always been close and now we bonded even more. And he treated Johnny to sports games. Thereafter, he was always available to help both of us with our grief.

After my father had passed, Mom had no choice but to get her driver's license. She learned to drive Dad's car so she could get around. She had been schoolmates with the present mayor, and he got Mom a full-time civil service job as a dispatcher at the Somerville Police station. She worked second-shift, from 3 p.m. to 11 p.m., which worked out well. While Mom was gone in the late afternoon and evenings, Johnny and I would come home from school and have dinner with my aunt, uncle and grandmother. It was a good way to retain the family bonds.

Mom and Nana Emma were old-fashioned Italians. They wore black for a full year. They also refused to watch TV or listen to the radio. Mom expected me to mourn the same way, and the two of us struggled over our differences. She thought I was disrespectful to my dad's memory, but

33

I stood my ground. I agreed to wear dark colors, but I would not wear nothing but black all the time. I never regretted my decision or felt guilty because Dad and I had had such a great relationship. He would have thought this excessive mourning was ridiculous.

Another bone of contention arose between me and Mom. She expected me to quit school to work full-time to help support her and Johnny. She also thought I should postpone the wedding, even though it was over a year away. I mustered my courage—inner strength from my Dad and God above, no doubt—to stand strong and say, "Absolutely not!" My dad knew when and where and who I was marrying and was thrilled for us. I had worked my ass off to become a teacher and I was almost done. I had good grades, doubled up on classes, and—come hell or high water—I was not changing my plans. It wasn't easy, but I stood tall and did not waver.

Nothing was the same without my dad. I missed him every day, but I appreciated that his suffering was over and that he was in a better place. I knew he was finally at peace, but I couldn't believe I would never again see his kind and gentle face. Kenny, too, had a hard time losing him. Dad had become a father figure of sorts to him, since his own father was mostly absent from the house, working long hours to support his large family. He seldom had time to spend with Kenny. My dad was gone but I was blessed to have Uncle Bob still, and so was Kenny.

Looking back, I realize I never had a chance to grieve for Dad on my own terms. Above my own needs, I had to be strong for Mom and brother, and I resented that. This has haunted me throughout my life.

Mom refused to come with me to choose a wedding gown because she was still in her bereavement time. My grandmother came instead and bought my dress. A friend from Saint Anthony's worked at House of Bianci in Boston, and she offered us a wholesale discount on her sample dresses. I fell in love with a beautiful designer gown, an A-line with a high neckline and long sleeves. Even better, it was in our price range, including the veil. I loved it and was so excited.

My favorite color was pink. These were the days of the "Age of Aquarius" counter-culture against tradition, Viet Nam war protests, LSD, and free love. Kenny and I paid no attention to the hippie culture, but we liked the new, electric-bright psychedelic colors. My maid of honor would be in hot pink and the bridesmaids in light pink. Back in the seventies, tuxes in all different colors outnumbered the black or white ones. Kenny decided to wear a white jacket, while the guys would wear pink ones. They all laughed and said, "It takes a *man* to wear pink!" Only for me would they have done this.

All year Mom frowned. She insisted that she would be sad all day at the wedding and she stood firm about that. (I'm almost surprised she didn't insist on wearing black to the wedding.)

My girlfriends surprised me with a bridal shower on March 17th, Saint Patrick's Day. I had been told that we were going to the soccer banquet of one of their boyfriends. Such beautiful gifts! We received everything we needed (and more!). Back then there was no bridal registry, so we ended up with four irons and three blenders, as well as other duplicates. We made several trips to Service Merchandise to make returns or exchanges.

Preparing the wedding list was a production. Kenny's family went over their quota. Mom presented me with a huge list of distant relatives I'd never even met. As usual, our mothers got what they wanted, forcing Kenny and me to scale down invitations to our own friends. To soothe me, Kenny said, "Never mind, let them have it their way for now. We'll do it our way, down the road." He reasoned that for our twenty-fifth wedding anniversary we'd have total control of the invitations to our party. (And we did! See **Chapter Four—Sheila**.)

Another dilemma arose: Who would walk me down the aisle? I chose Uncle Bob, but Mom insisted that it be my brother Johnny. I knew that would be a lot of pressure on Johnny. And besides, Uncle Bob was a father figure to me. But against my better judgment, I gave in. My uncle was disappointed, but he understood.

Although Kenny was slender and his father of a husky build, they always shared underwear, socks, and tops. Kenny's clothes were always stretched into shapelessness. So, whenever I saw anything on sale in Kenny's size, I bought it and stored it in new plastic bins. After we married, Kenny left his old clothes behind for his dad.

We also filled my hope chest with post-wedding going-away outfits and honeymoon attire. I bought peignoir sets and satin nightgowns. People bought us linens. We couldn't wait to find an apartment and finally live together, fall asleep together, and wake up in each other's arms. Like The Beach Boys sang, "Wouldn't it be nice to live together in the kind of world where we belong?"

Now came the home stretch to the wedding. We had paid off our furniture. We had enough money for the Newton Marriott for our wedding night and the honeymoon suite in The Poconos. I took Mom to choose her gown. Her year of mourning was over, and despite her attitude, I insisted on color. She wore turquoise, my grandmother and Kenny's mother wore pink, and my aunt wore coral.

By the end of March 1974, a month before the wedding, I had completed my academic work at Boston State, qualifying me for kindergarten to eighth grade. I began a 12-week student-teaching program at the new Kennedy School in Somerville, spending six weeks in second grade and six weeks in sixth grade. Working directly with children, I soon realized that young children were my passion. With everything else under control (sort of), I started interviewing for jobs in the fall. Not very far down the road now, Kenny and I would be making our new home together in a Somerville neighborhood.

CHAPTER THREE

Waldo

— — — — — — — — — — — — — —

Our wedding day was less than a month away. We rented an apartment from one of my co-workers, on Waldo Street right off of Highland Avenue. It had five rooms and finished attic space. It was convenient for me since I could take the bus or walk to local elementary schools where I was substitute-teaching. As promised, LaLa and Uncle Bob bought us a dining room set as a wedding gift. We spent hours cleaning and painting before moving in. We hung curtains and put away shower gifts, but still abided by our 10:30 and 11:00 p.m. curfews. Can you imagine how scared we were of getting in trouble? Our saving grace was that we would soon be living together, in our first apartment, legitimately, as husband and wife.

Mom was distraught that I was soon to move out, leaving her and my brother alone. Our apartment was only two miles away, but she tried to make me feel guilty for getting married. It did not work. We had done all the right things, were hard-working, responsible, helped our families, and achieved our goals. We had proved that we could always find a way to overcome every obstacle. It was exhausting, but so worth it. We deserved to be together and a chance at a better life for ourselves. We would now have the freedom to decide for ourselves what we wanted to do.

To her guilt trip, Mom had added a family visit – Mom, Johnny and me - on every holiday, special occasion, and Sunday to Mount Auburn Cemetery to visit the graves of my maternal grandfather and now my father. She forced the obligation and I hated it. Shortly before the wedding, Mom insisted that on the morning of my wedding day, I must go to the cemetery, fully dressed in my gown. I refused to crush what should be the happiest day of my life with such a visceral reminder that Dad was gone.

Let's just say that my refusal made things arduous for me. The night before my wedding I cried myself to sleep.

Our wedding date approached rapidly. Shortly before it, Kenny's grandmother ended up in Mass General with pneumonia and a bowel obstruction. We were so sad she had to miss our wedding. Everyone was going to miss her, too.

It was tradition then for the rehearsal dinner to be hosted at the bride's family home, rather than at a restaurant. Mom prepared and served sandwiches and desserts. She surprised me that she proved to be such a good hostess.

Although Kenny and I were young - I was twenty-one and Kenny had just turned twenty-two - we weren't nervous in the least about getting married. Our greater concern was how our families would blend at the reception, with alcohol mixed into the general chaos. The strict and conservative Cellis and the partying Rennells—what a combo! We hoped for the best!

On Sunday morning, April 28, 1974, our wedding day, Kenny went to the hospital to visit his grandmother. Needless to say, she was thrilled to see him in his tuxedo, so handsome! Here I share the Polaroid picture of them together.

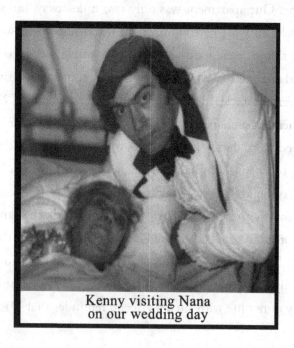

Kenny visiting Nana on our wedding day

Our wedding day was finally here! The day was spectacular, with a sun-filled sky and blooming spring flowers. My maid of honor, Jean, and my bridesmaids, Kenny's sister Linda and my friends Maria and Ann, came over to help me dress. The room was full of happy tension, as the photographer took pictures of this preparation for the wedding album. He captured us in every detail – applying lipstick in front of the mirror, adjusting my veil, pinning on my mother's corsage and my brother's boutonniere.

The limo came at last to deliver us to the church. We climbed up the church steps and entered the back of the nave, and saw all of our favorite people gathered for us. It was a dream come true! I couldn't believe it: Finally, I was a bride!

My future husband would be waiting for me at the raised altar at the front of the sanctuary. I couldn't wait to see him. We had talked on the phone in the morning, excited that the next time we saw each other, we would be exchanging our wedding vows.

It was time. The organist commenced with "Here Comes the Bride." At the altar Father Joe waited. To his left stood Kenny, his cousin Paul as his best man, and his cousin Dickie and my cousins Eddie and David as ushers. My bridesmaids advanced in front of us, then my maid of honor, with Johnny and me last.

Sure enough, I had eyes for no one else but my Kenny. He was a handsome man already, but even more so on this special day. When I reached him, his eyes were filled with joy and love. Although the church was filled, it seemed like we were the only two people in the room. After the formal proceedings, we exchanged wedding bands. Father Joe proclaimed us husband and wife. We turned to face the crowd and Father Joe introduced us as Mr. and Mrs. Kenneth Rennell!

It was music to our ears. The entire church exploded with applause. We ran happily down the aisle, hand in hand, and out to the limo, where we broke open the champagne and toasted our vows, and held each other close. "We did it!"

Our Wedding Day
April 28, 1974

On Our Honeymoon

Into the hall we came to jovial cheers from all. The traditional receiving line consisted of us two, our parents and all the bridesmaids and groomsmen. Our guests all offered their best wishes and congrats. Our first dance was to "Love is Blue," our song. Next came the cake cutting and the bouquet toss. We wore out our feet, dancing to the three-piece band with its female singer.

We had an amazing time and everything went great. Our fears about how well the Cellis and the Rennels would mingle went unfounded. Afterward, we changed into our going-away outfits and said our goodbyes. Everyone circled around us as we got into our Plymouth Duster, newly decorated with "Just Married" posters. (Kenny had given strict instructions to use only streamers. He didn't want dangling tin cans to scratch his car's pristine blue paint job. He was quite the fanatic about his cars.) And off we drove to the Newton Marriott for our first time in a hotel together. We were silly and giddy. It was a magical night.

1970 PLYMOUTH DUSTER 340

The next morning, we set out, down the road, on the six-hour drive to The Poconos, our first road trip as newlyweds. We talked all the way about all the hurdles we had overcome. He revealed that he felt bad only about leaving behind his sister Paula, his buddy, and Chippa, his shepherd-lab-mix dog, Chippa. But we'd be back with them soon.

The honeymoon resort was nestled in the mountains, with cottages and hotel-like rooms, interspersed between red-and-pink covered bridges. It was our own little piece of paradise. We stayed in a bungalow (a private unit, cheaper than the suites), quaint with a decor of hearts and cupids, and we loved everything about it.

Our honeymoon was a most romantic week. I felt safe and secure with him and we looked forward to a life of love and happiness. I will spare you the details; that is for another book. We enjoyed all the activities for newlyweds—music, dance, and adult games. The late-April weather cooperated so we could hike, play tennis, and take long nature walks. Participation was optional, and "Do Not Disturb" signs were available for private times. Our sign was tattered and torn by the end of the week.

One dispute throughout our marriage was gun ownership. Kenny had a license to carry a weapon, belonged to a gun club, and hunted. I was uncomfortable around guns, but I quickly learned that this dilemma was not negotiable. He believed in learning gun safety and he enjoyed the sport. Much to my dismay one of the activities on the honeymoon schedule was skeet shooting. Despite my apprehension and to support his interest, I shot my first gun on our honeymoon – badly, of course. Kenny, on the other hand, won a first-prize trophy. What were the chances?

While we were in Pennsylvania, Kenny scoped out two junkyards he knew about. We went shopping there and bought a number of parts for his old '56 Chevy. Leave it to us!

Linda at the range   Kenny at the range
Skeet Shooting in The Poconos

Although we were sad to leave The Poconos, we were eager to return home to begin married life. We were both suckers for tradition, so Kenny carried me over the threshold to our new home. Our apartment was fully furnished and crammed with all the shower and wedding gifts. Once we put all that in order, the apartment was adorable. Kenny and I found pure joy living together as husband and wife in our own place.

I continued my day job as a substitute teacher, and Kenny continued his work at Polaroid on the graveyard shift, from 11 p,m. to 7 a.m. Of course, that meant I went to bed after he went to work. I never had slept in a house by myself before, but I sucked it up and got used to it. I always brightened at the idea that he'd soon come through the door while I got ready to leave for work. We shared our late afternoons and evenings, had dinner together, and watched TV. We made it work. We both worked Saturdays, too, so our only full day together was Sunday. I had never cooked or done laundry before, but I quickly became domesticated. I loved being his wife!

My graduation from Boston State College was held a few weeks after our honeymoon, at the Hynes Auditorium in Boston. What a whirlwind! I dressed in my cap and gown at our apartment, proud of this huge accomplishment. After taking family pictures, we headed to the ceremony. It was great to be with all of my friends and family, especially now with my husband by my side. As I walked across the stage with my diploma in hand, Kenny cheered loudly from the audience. My heart was full of joy. A part of it ached for my other cheerleader—Dad—but I knew he watched from above, bursting with pride.

| Kenny and I | My mother, me, |
| at my graduation | and my brother Johnny |

Linda E. Rennell

In September of 1974, I got my first full-time teaching job as a Title I remedial reading teacher for first through third grades. Although it was part of the Somerville public school system, the classroom was in Saint Anthony's parochial school with the nuns. Kenny's former Mother Superior was now my boss.

It was at this job that I met my aide, Rosemarie, nicknamed "Ro," who was re-entering the workforce after an absence. She and I made a great team and worked well together. We quickly became friends. Our two years of teaching together forged a permanent friendship.

We did lose touch for a while, at different stages of our lives, but Ro reached out to me after her husband, Ron, passed away of stomach cancer. During our senior years, we have become sisters by choice.

Rosemarie and I
enjoying lunch together

Polaroid laid off Kenny shortly after I landed my job. For a while he collected unemployment and worked some remodeling jobs with a construction company owned by Al, the husband of my high school friend

Debbie. We socialized a lot with them and took day trips in Al's Ford Mustang. Eventually, Kenny got a call-back to Polaroid, thank God!

Although we loved our first apartment, we were uncomfortable with the behavior of our landlords' ten-year-old son and the boy's grandmother. She slept in the cellar, which was dingy and smelled musty. The son played weird games and made loud noises. I noticed these things because the landlord allowed us to use the washer and dryer, which were in the cellar. The behaviors of the boy and the grandmother were odd and made me uneasy. Thereafter I did laundry only when Kenny was home.

Disaster struck in 1976 on the Friday of February school vacation. Kenny was away at his 3-11 shift at Polaroid, so I was home alone. The winter day was cold and raw, the ground covered with week-old snow. I was under the hairdryer when I saw Rusty, an awesome long-haired orange cat we had adopted, arch his back and pace anxiously, which was out of character for him. Then I heard a fire engine. In a moment, two firefighters with axes were chopping down my front door. Then I smelled smoke. The house was on fire! I grabbed Rusty and ran outside, dressed only in my robe and slippers.

A neighbor alerted Kenny and he raced home in disbelief. I called my family and they came right over. We all watched the destruction, heartbroken. The house was clad in vinyl siding, which directed the flames up the inside of the walls and through the roof. It was awful to see all of our new furniture and belongings thrown out the windows, ruined. All of the salvageable furniture had to be put in an ozone chamber to eliminate the stink of smoke. All the sheetrock and insulation were water-soaked. The authorities investigated the fire. Apparently, they found it suspicious, but no proof of how it started. I always wondered if the landlord's son or the grandmother had anything to do with it. We were out of a home, but grateful that no one had been hurt.

We took shelter at my mother's house until we could figure out what to do. (You can only imagine how that went!) The night after that chaos,

Kenny said we would never go back to that apartment, we would buy our own house. Although I was overwhelmed with the stress, he was so confident that I couldn't help but believe him.

Shortly before the fire, Kenny's godmother, Esther, his cousin Paul's mother, was diagnosed with pancreatic cancer. Kenny and I were close to her and her husband, Uncle Paul. She had always been like a mother to Kenny, watching out for him. She suffered greatly with the cancer and became very sick. A month after the fire she passed away. Another loss for us. She was a marvelous lady and we all missed her dearly.

Kenny, Paul, and Dickie were first cousins, Kenny the youngest and Dickie the oldest. They called themselves The Three Amigos. Dickie and Linda (the Volpicellis) were already married, living in Bedford, and Paul and Carol (the Stratis) had married the year after us and lived in Burlington. The six of us spent weekends together and had lots of fun, so Kenny and I looked for a house near them.

| The Three Amigos: cousins Dickie, Kenny, & Paul | Three Amigos' Wives: Linda, Carol, & me |

After we moved in with my mother, we settled into a routine. My brother Johnny was now in high school, playing baseball and football. Mom still worked for the Somerville Police Station. I taught during the day and Kenny worked the 3-11 shift. In the daytime Mom and Kenny were home, and at night I was home, often helping Johnny with his homework.

While I was at work, Kenny went house-hunting. We considered nearby Woburn, about halfway between Somerville and Tewksbury where our families lived. Initially we planned to buy a fixer-upper, since he was handy and we could make it our own. The difference between an older house and a new house was usually about $7,000 -$8,000, a lot of money then.

One day Kenny came across a new development in Woburn with a lot for sale. So then we discussed building a new house and decided to go for it. We preferred a split-level design. We could build out the first-floor living quarters first, so we could move in, and then Kenny could finish the downstairs as we could afford it. The idea of having a mortgage was exciting and scary, but we knew how to work hard to meet the payments. Already, in the year and a half since we married, with both of us working full-time and part-time jobs, we had saved about $10,000.

Mom flipped out about us moving so far away. But Nana Emma was happy for us. She really bailed us out. She lent us another $10,000 to reduce our mortgage payment. We promised to pay her back before we started a family, and we did.

Off we went, down the road, to the next chapter of our lives—as homeowners!

CHAPTER 4

Sheila

- - - - - - - - - - - - - - -

The parcel of land where we built our house used to be part of Spence Farm. This landmark had been a well-known farm with a vegetable and fruit stand and a nursery. The lot very close to the Burlington-Woburn town line, just west of Central Square. Conservation land and wetlands abutted our lot, making it very private.

It was exciting to watch the foundation, the framing, the sheetrock, and the plastering grow into what became our home. We visited the site at least once a week to watch the construction. From home-improvement catalogs we chose kitchen cabinets, vanities, counter tops, harvest-gold appliances, and windows. The clapboards were apple-green, accented with white shutters. We upgraded the model to hardwood floors and electrical service downstairs. We even got a garage and a fireplace. For heat, we chose forced hot water over hot air. Kenny had a deviated septum in his nose, so he needed moist air to prevent nosebleeds. And we created a journal of dozens of Polaroids photos to record how the shell became a house.

In July 1976 we moved into our new home on 6 Sheila Avenue in Woburn, Massachusetts. It was only the second house in the development, on a dirt road. It didn't even have street lights yet. Little by little, we made improvements to the house. Kenny bought a bird bath, bird houses, and wind chimes. We planted shrubs and trees in the front. Paul helped Kenny install a cement patio under our deck. And little by little, neighbors built on other lots and moved in, young couples like us, beginning their lives together. We befriended them. Everything was great.

I continued teaching Title I Preschool in Somerville and took up private tutoring of math for extra money. I still worked days and Kenny still worked the 3-to-11 shift. It was comforting to have him home at the night.

After we moved to Woburn, we were in the habit of returning to Somerville for most of our errands and appointments. Eventually we shifted our banking, shopping, and errands to Woburn. Living in Woburn required a car for my commute. My first car was a new 1976 light-blue Buick. This added a car payment to our financial obligations, of course, but we loved our country atmosphere. Having lived in urban Somerville, we were used to the sound of fire trucks, police, and ambulances. Now all we heard were crickets or dead silence. We loved to sit together, out on the deck, and sip tea.

Rusty the cat still lived with us, but we wanted a dog, too. We took a trip to the Boston Animal Shelter and came home with an adorable brown-and-white Sheltie pup. She was called Spunky and she definitely lived up to her name. She was a masterful digger and an escape artist. Kenny had always had dogs, so he trained her. I had always wanted a puppy, so I was thrilled. She was great company and always greeted us with a waggy tail and unconditional love. We were pleased that she and Rusty became friends, too.

Along came the famous Blizzard of '78, which paralyzed the entire Northeast for over a week. The storm dumped over two feet of snow on top of the two feet already on the ground that January had left behind. The snow piled in towering drifts capped by an icy crust that made it impossible to move. We ended up house-bound for close to a month. We cooked, cleaned and watched lots of TV when we had power. We walked the streets and hung out with neighbors and friends. Spunky quickly came to love playing in the snow.

With hard work we saved money and paid back my grandmother's loan. Kenny worked hard finishing our downstairs. He completed the laundry room with cabinets and a countertop. He built a brick bar in a family room, which came out awesome. We spent endless hours together deciding where walls should go, designing the specific areas with sheet rock. The walls were covered with light brown paneling. He also added a bathroom downstairs with a walk-in shower stall. We worked as a team, me on the interior design and Kenny on the landscaping. We wallpapered walls, laid down carpeting, hung wall hangings and pictures. Kenny planted annual and perennial flowers in planting beds around the house, protecting them with bark mulch.

Kenny's ability to master any project always had me in disbelief; there was nothing he couldn't do. I was proud of his work, and we loved to entertain family and friends in our newly finished downstairs.

Eventually our house was finished, inside and out. Financially we were solvent, meeting the mortgage and monthly bills easily. We contemplated starting a family, but Kenny really needed a new car. His Plymouth Duster had racked up the miles and it needed major repairs. I suggested that he do so while we still had two incomes. His dream car was a Pontiac Trans Am. He ordered a gold-colored one with a magnificent black phoenix sprawling on its hood scoop. It was gorgeous. He always worked so hard, he deserved it.

1978 Trans Am

On one of our vacations, we took our first trip out of the country, to Montreal, Canada. Disco was big at that time. We had taken dance lessons with friends, so we hit the clubs and strutted our stuff under glittering disco balls that summer.

In the fall we discovered that I was pregnant. I figured that since I wasn't due until the next June, I could easily work the entire school year. Late in the pregnancy, however, toxemia set in, which made working more challenging than expected. But I made it past Memorial Day, 1979.

Back then, everyone went to childbirth classes. I arranged to deliver at Cambridge Hospital where my gynecologist practiced. I was huge! I underwent one of the first ultrasounds to see if I was carrying twins. Nope! It was just one big baby!

In April we signed up for a six-week session of night classes. With my size, I kidded Kenny that I would not sit near some skinny girl who had only gained fifteen pounds. I'd look for someone with a belly as big as mine to befriend. Sure enough, I spotted Lorraine and Lee Benoit. Her belly looked just like mine. Lee was super-friendly and had a great sense of humor. We became lifelong friends and are still like family.

On June 2, 1979, Eric Rennell came into the world via C-section, weighing ten pounds and two ounces, and measuring twenty-two inches long. Lorraine and Lee Benoits' son, T.J., arrived three weeks later. We were blessed two years later when our daughter, Monica, was born. They were blessed with three more sons.

We loved being parents. Eric was awesome, an easy baby. Sucking on his pacifier, the child charmed us with his big brown eyes. At two weeks he weighed twelve pounds and was already eating cereal. He was always hungry but seldom slept. He was not a great napper but he smiled all day long. Kenny and I agreed that I would stay home with Eric, and soon I was providing home daycare for the children of a few of my teacher friends. I found myself really enjoying the work with these infants and toddlers. We spent time outside a lot, doing art projects and playing games. I loved being a wife and mother!

It wasn't long before Baby Number Two was on the way. This pregnancy was the other extreme of my first. Unlike when carrying Eric, I was sick almost every day for the whole nine months. Was I glad when Monica Lynn joined our family on November 9, 1981! She weighed in at eight pounds and measured twenty inches. Despite the discomfort of my second pregnancy, Kenny and I were thrilled to have both a healthy boy and a healthy girl! We were in love with our little family.

Monica proved to be the opposite of Eric in many ways. She slept through the night early and napped well, but was feisty when awake. Our handsome son was bald and our precious daughter had a headful of dark hair. Eric's looks took after me (although I wasn't bald), and Monica's looks took after Kenny.

Once Monica came along, I could no longer do daycare. Kenny worked as much overtime at Polaroid as he could get, and picked up a second job a couple of nights a week. I felt bad about the burden on him, but with only one income money was tight. On those two nights a week, I would pack food and the kids, and we'd bring dinner to Kenny. He was always happy and grateful to see us and we made good family-time memories together.

Kenny was always a hard worker and never complained; he did what needed to be done. He was so reliable that I never worried that he could provide for us. He always followed through and got things done. Our families never had much and as most parents do, we wanted better for our children. Our ambition and drive always motivated us.

Every Fourth of July we spent at Uncle Paul's with cousins Dianne and Jay, Paul and Carol, and Dickie and Linda, along with all kinds of other family members. There were babies and kids everywhere. The poolside was lined with high chairs and play pens. The Strati yards were side by side and were full of seasonal flowers. There were gigantic vegetable gardens abounding with tomato, cucumber and zucchini plants. It was great to see all the cousins interact and enjoy themselves. At first, there were about a dozen girls and only two boys, but eventually more males came along. The horseshoe competition, bocci and volley ball games were the highlight of the day. All aspired to get their names etched onto Uncle Paul's homemade wooden trophy.

We were so lucky that the Stratis, Kenny's uncle and cousins, always included Kenny and me and our kids in these holiday gatherings. These people were his mother Rita's family and Kenny had not had a close relationship with his parents for years.

The annual Christmas Party was always held the Sunday before Christmas at Paul and Carol's house. Their home was beautiful and was decorated for Christmas inside and outside. Paul's yearly mission was to find a fourteen-foot, perfectly shaped tree to adorn with family ornaments and hundreds of lights. Santa Claus always visited to hand out presents, and we always had a Yankee swap and a family sing-along. We broke up into groups for "The Twelve Days of Christmas." Auntie Linda was always our family conductor. Through the years, as the family grew, so did attendance, up to about seventy.

Cousins and wives on the Fourth of July

Kenny's work-shift changed to days, from 7:00 to 3:30, so he was home by 4:00 p.m. I took up tutoring local kids again, part-time after school in algebra and geometry. This gave me a break from our kids and I got a paycheck. Win-win! When Kenny came home, I'd go to work, and Kenny got time alone with the kids. By the time I returned home, around 7:30 p.m., he would have fed them and given them baths. We always enjoyed our family weekend time together, whether it was walks at Horn Pond, bike riding, or day trips with cousins and friends. Life was busy but wonderful.

Eric had always been a healthy child. But one April morning, while Monica was still asleep in her crib, he said he felt sick when he got up. He was a little warm to my touch, so I laid him down on the couch in the living room and went to the kitchen to get him a cup of apple juice. When I got back, he was having a seizure. Even though I was first-aid and CPR trained, I panicked. I picked him up and tipped him on his side and frantically called 911. By the time I heard the deluge of loud sirens, the seizure had subsided. The paramedics came in and checked his temperature, and it had spiked to 103 degrees. We were off in the ambulance before I knew it. It was my first ride ever in an ambulance, and the paramedics were so kind to both of us.

In the emergency, I almost forgot about Monica. My neighbor stayed with her and Kenny met me at the emergency room. I felt absolutely helpless seeing my baby boy on a stretcher in the ER.

The hospital kept him for a few days. The diagnosis was an inner-ear infection that caused a sudden hike in temperature, triggering a febrile seizure. His pediatrician prescribed phenobarbital, which was controversial at the time. But we trusted her and it worked. He was on the prescription for two years, and eventually outgrew the condition.

Another time Eric got pneumonia and had a 104-degree temperature. God bless Kenny! He took Eric with him into a cold-water bath or shower to bring down the temperature, and we dosed the tyke with Tylenol.

Regretfully this process did not work, and Eric spent a week in a plastic oxygen tent in the hospital. Poor little guy was so scared! Kenny and I alternated nights staying with him, but it was brutal for all of us. Thankfully he recovered perfectly, but it was a frightening episode. On those rare occasions when Eric got ill, it was always serious.

Monica struggled with chronic ear infections. In the early 1980s, tubes for drainage were not a common course of action for children's ear infections, so she was prescribed antibiotics. With those, she bounced back quickly.

As the kids grew, their extracurricular activities became our social life. Preschool, t-ball, soccer, birthday parties, playgroups, and dance lessons kept us very busy. Eric started preschool around the same time that most of our cousins' and friends' kids did. Through the kids we made new friends and blended into the community. We loved every minute of it.

Eric, age 4 & Monica, age 2

Kenny restored cars as a hobby. There was always at least one undergoing different stages of rebuild, every aspect of which he loved with a passion. But he selflessly offered to sell his Trans Am and '56 Chevy to buy a swimming pool for the kids. Lee and Kenny installed a round, above-ground pool with a deck, ran wiring for the filter, and installed lights in the shed we added to store pool supplies. Kenny was not fond of swimming but the kids loved it. He tested the water regularly and added the chemicals so it was always crystal clear. On hot summer weekends Kenny hung out on the deck with us and sometimes jumped in to cool off. We spent most summer days poolside.

A deck fence surrounded the pool, but we also needed a perimeter fence around the yard. On one weekend, Lee and Kenny worked all day Saturday and Sunday, digging holes for the posts and installing a four-foot-high picket fence. Lee's wife Lorraine and I hung around inside with our children and made lunch, snacks, drinks, and supper to keep us all going.

I had volunteered to paint the fence white when they were done. I clearly bit off more than I could chew. The next week I painted and painted and painted. Eric ran around the yard and Monica squirmed in her stroller. At day's end, I had finished only two sections of it. I admitted that I needed help, so we invited friends and family for a paint party. Ten paint brushes are better than one. Lee never let me live it down! We still laugh about it today.

Once both of the kids were in school full days, we did better financially. Kenny had sacrificed so much in selling his muscle cars, so he really wanted another classic car. He wanted the kids to share his interest in cars. Kenny always had something cool going on. He found a 1931 Ford two-seater hot rod in Fort Lauderdale, Florida, in The Want Ad book. He called the owner, who mailed us a VCR tape of it. It was purplish-pink and chopped low to the ground. We bought it.

It came on a car carrier about three weeks later, on a nice spring day. The kids had friends over at our house and they were equally excited about the hot rod's arrival. It made us the talk of the neighborhood. We had fun taking it to lots of car shows. Kenny kept it for a few years, then traded it for a 1955 Chevy. After he did some much-needed body work and a new paint job, it became his favorite car!

1931 Ford Hot Rod

We often got together with cousin Paul and Carol with their children Mark, Chrissy and Steph, and with cousin Dickie and Linda and their children, Kara, Nicole and Richie. We went to Disney on Ice, Children's Museum, the New England Aquarium, Hampton Beach Day, and all the kid-friendly local events. We enjoyed cookouts and beach days with our friends Maria and Frank. Their kids, Maura and Brian, were almost the same age as ours. The boys played baseball and soccer, and the girls danced at the same studio and competed together. Eric was a natural athlete and Monica loved to dance. Between Eric's sports-team travels and Monica's solos and competitions, we were always busy.

After Monica's birth, our dog Spunky became very jealous and would chew the kids' toys. Sometimes she even nipped at the kids, so we had to have another family adopt her. Kenny and I were sad to give her up, but Eric and Monica's safety had to be our top priority.

Eric begged us for a puppy for his eighth birthday. After assessing the proposal, we found a cute black lab-shepherd-mix puppy. Uncle Bob had seen her at a truck stop in Connecticut. We named her Chippa after the beloved dog Kenny had in his teens. She loved running around the yard in circles and playing with the kids. Chasing a tennis ball was her favorite game and whenever Kenny pulled into the driveway, she ran to find one. Chippa would catch high flies until she collapsed. She was gentle with us, but fiercely protective.

We took Eric to Amherst for a soccer tournament and to Cooperstown for baseball. We did a family trip to Florida where Monica danced on the Americana Stage in Disney World. We were so proud of both of them and all of their accomplishments. I was the nurturing and protective one and Kenny raised them to be fearless and independent. Like most couples, we had our share of arguments over forms and levels of discipline, but the fruits of our labor paid off. We must have done something right, because they were both amazing. It was evident how both of our personalities intertwined in both of them. How lucky we were!

Monica
Disney's DANCE magazine cover

Eric
Disney's SPORT magazine cover

Kenny was handy and he decided that we ought to buy a duplex in Woburn, an investment for extra income. I decided to go back to teaching, but I didn't want to work in the public school system. I wanted to own my own private preschool for three-, four-, and five-year-olds. It was tough to figure out how we could both get what we wanted.

I was nervous about owning a residential rental property and the responsibilities of being landlords. God forbid we should ever have to evict a family with children! I couldn't imagine us doing that. At first, I thought it would be best to build an addition onto our home to house my preschool, but Kenny was reluctant. He was afraid, wisely I believe now, that when it closed for the day or the weekend, it would be impossible for me to set down the business obligations.

We compromised and agreed to buy a commercial property for my school. I would run the school and Kenny would continue working at Polaroid. On weekends he would clean, landscape, and do the basic maintenance at the school. It sounded like a great idea and we both became excited with this new direction.

What town did I want to open the school in, Kenny asked. I wanted Woburn because it would be close to home. Woburn lacked a private, part-time preschool (as did other towns), not a daycare. I preferred a Main Street location, but in a residential zone, not a commercial zone.

We would need two loans, one to buy a property and one to cover construction and renovation costs. We talked to both small local banks and larger regional banks, but none would risk taking us on. All we had for collateral was our home. Plus, we had no previous small-business experience. They all said we had to find a financial investment partner.

It seemed that our dream was shattered. But Kenny promised to find a way. He found a potential business partner from Weymouth who was looking to invest in a property. The fellow owned his own construction company and wanted to start building in the North Shore. We thought our prayers were answered, and for a while, they were.

The day after Thanksgiving we packed up the kids with coloring books, crayons and markers, bundled into the car, and drove to Weymouth to meet our new partner. We told no one else about the business meeting. The man confirmed that he had his own attorney, accountant, and bookkeeper, all of whom had offices in his Weymouth building. We were very impressed. He would be the contractor and agreed to build the preschool. We would own 100% of the preschool, and he would be a 50/50 partner in the building until we bought him out as the property developed equity. It sounded too good to be true.

Kenny was the researcher of the pair. He went on a mission to find appropriate properties available in Woburn. After checking out a few, Kenny found a two-family in North Woburn that was zoned business-highway. It was in a homey neighborhood near Route 128 and Route 93. It looked like a dump to me, but Kenny had the foresight to envision the property's potential.

Located on an acre of land, it had been an historical dwelling, so there were some local zoning restrictions. The plan was to gut it out and get a construction loan to build new. Although I was nervous about it, Kenny was all for it. Our partner came to see the location and concurred that this was a good site for our new venture. We bought the property in November of 1986, floating on our partner's financial statement and his experience. We had to hurry to get it built before the following September, at the beginning of the school year. We got a construction loan and broke ground in January,1987.

Our partner's architect had designed a daycare for his previous employer and he worked with us on blueprints. Kenny knew how to read the prints and we pored over them together. Originally, we talked about a single-story building to house the preschool, but our partner advised us that it was cheaper in the long run to build up. He added a second floor to gain rental income for himself. I handled the interior design and Kenny handled acquiring permits and hiring subcontractors.

When we first began to talk about this, I contacted the Department for Children (now The Office of Early Education and Care) in Waltham to determine the Massachusetts licensing process. I found out about square-footage requirements for preschool students. I went to the department meetings to learn the state regulations. Knowledge is power. I plowed forward for almost a year to get my provisional, six-month license, necessary before I could obtain eligibility for a two-year state license later.

I called one of my best friends, Maria, a former teacher with a degree in Early Childhood Education. I shared my plan and offered her the position of assistant director. She was on board as soon as I asked.

The new preschool needed a name. I liked double letters and wanted something simple that students could remember. I had no idea how complicated it would be to find a good name. I came up with Smart Starters, but that was unavailable, already registered by a preschool on Cape Cod. Back to the drawing board. After thinking about it more, I decided that the name should be symbolic of a preschool's qualities. I realized that "wonder" is an elemental building block of learning. Thus was born "World of Wonder." Our logo was a globe!

Luckily, I had worked in Somerville's Project Smile and was on a Curriculum Revision Committee. Title One was a federally funded program and its teachers were involved in the educational process. I developed three levels of curriculum: 3-year-old (Nursery), 4-year-old (Pre-K) and 5-year-old (Transition). I carried a journal with me everywhere and kept one on my nightstand to jot down ideas. Maria and I met periodically to develop courses of study. After about six months we had the curricula written with age-appropriate math, social studies, art, science, music, and language arts.

Maria and I created classroom schedules and developed a multitude of written materials, like monthly newsletters, staff contracts, state preschool policies, staff and parent handbooks, and manuals on how to conduct classroom observations and prepare annual reviews.

Early in my career I had worked with a bright young director who said that blocks are the most important teaching tool for every preschool classroom. You can teach most skills with them (math, science, fine-motor). I kept that in mind and made sure my five classrooms had an ample supply of building block sets - Lego plastic bricks, wooden blocks, foam blocks, etc. She was right!

I enrolled in a night-school business class at Woburn High to familiarize myself with spreadsheets and financial issues. It didn't take long for me to realize the school needed a payroll service and a bookkeeper.

The next step was to apply for a small-business loan to fund our materials, equipment, and furnishings. Maria and I compiled a list of what the school needed—classroom chairs, desks, tables and other furniture, bulletin boards, manipulatives, fine- and gross-motor materials, books, blocks, creative-play areas, and playground equipment. I soon learned all about going to banks, filling out paperwork galore, meeting with contractors. I've always loved a challenge.

One day Kenny came home from work, proudly bearing two poster boards rolled up under his arm. On his lunch break he often drove around Waltham, exploring. That day he found an inspirational poster about following your dream. He bought one for our house and one for my new office. Thirty-three years later, the office one still hangs in World of Wonder's front hallway.

'Follow Your Dream' poster

Since I lived only two miles up the road, I met with the project manager daily to handle various modifications to accommodate the new situations that always popped up. I must say this project was The Talk of the Town! There was a lot of gossip about World of Wonder coming soon. People began calling me about a job, although I barely advertised. I interviewed local teachers, aides, a bookkeeper, and a nurse to join our staff. Hiring was easier than I thought it would be. It was essential to get background checks and to know personalities. The concept of teacher and aide teaming together relies on compatible temperaments and teaching styles. Luckily most of my staff lived in the city or abutting towns. They were local people with great qualifications and were as excited about this new preschool as we were.

We began enrolling students. Word of mouth, a little advertising in the local paper, and leaving flyers at the local library and elementary schools were our only marketing tools. As a preschool, not a daycare, we enrolled no infants or toddlers. Our teachers had bachelor degrees, a novelty at that time. We were brand-new, so people were taking a chance on us.

We had a big Open House and about a hundred families came, including local clergy, politicians and local public teachers. Our family friend, Lee, dressed up as a clown and handed out balloons. We offered refreshments and gave tours. Everyone was impressed with the classrooms, especially the fact that each room had its own sink for hand-washing and toddler-level potties for toilet-training. The offices looked professional with their desks and file cabinets. The event was amazing and received great publicity in the local newspaper.

By the skin of our teeth, we opened in September of 1987 with forty-five students and a staff of ten. Kenny was in charge of maintenance. The teachers and I would leave him a punch list and he handled it efficiently. He never complained and was more than capable of fixing anything we asked for. He was such a hard worker. It took a while for each of us to get what we wanted, but I got my school and Kenny got his investment property.

We both worked diligently to make this new endeavor a success. We took pride in the community service to families that we provided, in the city that we called home, where we were raising our own children. We ran an eight-week summer camp to help pay our rent towards the mortgage and all went well.

Our partner finished most of the second floor and found a dance studio to rent upstairs. The woman who owned Dance Productions – a tenant like me - was a first-time business owner, too. We were two women running small businesses and the building was full of children, learning and exercising—it was perfect! The preschool was open in the mornings and the dance studio was open in the late afternoon, nights, and Saturdays, so parking and acoustics were not a problem. Often our clientele overlapped with children learning downstairs and dancing upstairs. I displayed her flyers on my parent bulletin board and she distributed my pamphlets.

By the second year, WOW had almost one hundred students and still open only in the mornings. In Dance Production's second year, she had two hundred students. The following year I had two hundred students and she had three hundred. As enrollment increased, World of Wonder added three afternoons a week and we had a waiting list to get in! Yeah! Our two women-owned small businesses were flourishing.

It was at this time that I decided we needed a bigger kitchen and TV room at home. Kenny wanted more garage space (at the time we only had one) to work on his vehicles. We went to the Boston Home Show and met a architect-contractor from the South Shore whom we liked, who had his own subcontractors. He consulted with us and reviewed our wish list and came up with the blueprints. This time I knew how to read them!

He began work in March of 1995. Our goal was for him to finish by September so we'd be back indoors before snow flew. During the summer months we could grill outside. The kids begged us to put in central air conditioning but Kenny was opposed. He loved to have the windows open in nice weather and did not want the house to be all closed up. Settling for a whole-house attic fan was a compromise, but the kids and I still sweated during humid days and nights. Kenny was the guy who seldom perspired and hardly ever needed to wear deodorant. The construction schedule hit a few snags, but overall, things went smoothly, and our additions and renovations were mostly complete by early October.

I now had a huge kitchen with an island, a TV room off the kitchen, and a larger deck. Kenny got three more garages, one more out front and two in the back. Our original twenty-six by forty-four-foot house was now thirty-two-hundred square feet, with all-new champagne-colored siding and maroon shutters. The varied roof lines and front columns made our house look regal. Kenny had his Chevy Tahoe, which he used for daily driving, and his 1955 Chevy, and Eric had a Chevelle. My car was in the original front garage. No sooner was the project done than all four garages were occupied. We loved the addition and now could host all the holidays!

Our partner owned several commercial buildings and condos. Our 905 Main Street address was his smallest venture. When the condo market tumbled a few years later, things dramatically changed. He used monies from our building to finance and finish his other properties. Things fell apart quickly for us. Our utilities, taxes, and mortgage weren't getting paid. Our partner refused to answer our phone calls. Simply put, the property was heading to foreclosure. World of Wonder was prospering, however, so we decided to stop the foreclosure and take over full ownership of the property. After court depositions, litigations, and legal fees, we did so in 1996.

This stressful time confirmed that our marriage and our commitment to each other was unshakable. Our former partner's name was no longer on the deed. We created Monrica Realty Trust to own the property, named after our children. We never again needed another partner. Our persistence paid off.

* * *

The Antics of World of Wonder—Out of the Mouths of Babes (and Parents)

Owning and running a preschool was a new adventure every day. Here are samples of some crazy things that happened through the thirty years I owned the preschool:

❖ When a parent found a cigarette butt in the driveway, a teacher was accused of smoking on the playground. It turns out that it was dropped by a parent upstairs.

❖ During an enrichment program of Mother Goose, the performer fell asleep while on her break and I had to wake her up for her next performance.

❖ We hired a reptile program to come with small animals and he came with a boa constrictor around his neck.

❖ When we had an animal show and at lunch break they put their goat in our basement. When the teachers were eating it kicked and banged at the door.

❖ One of our mothers was pregnant and after summer break, I saw her out and about. I said, "Still waiting for your baby to come?" and she said, "I had a baby girl a month ago." I wanted to die!

❖ We called a dad into the office because his son constantly said, "F___ you" to his classmates. Dad thought his son exhibited strong leadership qualities. He believed that this behavior would help his son climb the corporate ladder.

❖ We had to conference with a parent about their child's aggressive behavior with his peers. His mother said she never saw him be physical. On the way out of the school he was whacking his mother with his backpack.

❖ When touring the preschool, a parent told me she wanted her son to have a place to play, but didn't need any academics. No way would or could I guarantee that. Clearly, she did not realize that children learn both academically and socially on a daily basis.

❖ When parents brought their child to visit, they thought the youngster was required to perform their ABCs and count to ten, as if it were an admissions test.

❖ At dismissal we asked a four-year-old student what color car his mother drove. I thought he said a Subaru. Then when his mother pulled up to our pick-up area, in a rusted-out car, he shouted out, "A shitbox." I stood corrected!

❖ During circle time, a student told her teacher that her mother locked her bedroom door when her Uncle Tom had a sleepover.

❖ A nursery teacher realized that one of her little girls was not wearing underwear. When she asked her why, the child said, "When I poop in my pants, my mother throws my underwear away and she forgets to buy more."

❖ One little boy always used to say, "I smell a fart! Is my dear uncle here?"

❖ When her aide told her to do something, a four-year-old responded, "My mother said I don't have to listen to you. I can do whatever I want!"

❖ When singing a seasonal song, a student shouted out, "Please, stop! I hate singing!" and covered his ears."

❖ When practicing for graduation, a preschooler said, "Why are we doing this—it is stupid!"

❖ A little girl with separation anxiety cried for her mother in my office. She asked me to drive her home and I said I didn't have a car that day, that it was being repaired. She said, "I don't care. I'll walk home!"

A sense of humor is a must, because every day at a preschool is a new experience!

* * *

For our 25th wedding anniversary, Kenny and I renewed our vows. This time we did it our way. We had a mass at Saint Anthony's with our pastor, Father Lynch, officiating. We invited all of the special people in our lives to the reception at a local hotel. Kenny wore a tux, as handsome as ever, and I wore a long dress. We even had an ice sculpture. We spent our second honeymoon in Las Vegas. Mission accomplished!

Eric and Monica were in high school now and doing very well. In his senior year, Eric became Captain of the Woburn Tanner Football team and was recruited to play either football or baseball in college. Since our construction of the building at 905 Main Street, he was always intrigued with architecture. He took drafting in high school and did well. He planned to go to Northeastern as an architect major and try out for the football team. In his senior year of high school, however, he was cleated at the plate during a baseball game, and his injury ruptured a pilonidal cyst in his back. He still attended Northeastern, but his injury prevented him from playing football.

Eric found that he did not like the huge university atmosphere with its large lecture halls. He transferred to Wentworth Institute of Technology in Boston, majoring in Project Management. There, he played baseball. His baseball practice and games as a catcher, his heavy-duty studies, and the long bus rides to various colleges became too much to juggle, however, so he gave up baseball in his junior year to focus on his academics.

He met Karen at Wentworth, who became his wife. She was in the same major, so they worked on projects together. Eric's GPA went up when they started dating and hers went down. She taught him to study and he taught her to have more fun! She is great!

Monica left dancing since this commitment on the competition team was too demanding. This allegiance had prohibited her from participating in other activities. She wanted to experience a team sport, so in high school she played field hockey. She applied to several local colleges and Merrimack College was her first choice. Initially she wanted to be a social worker, but ended up double-majoring in Sociology and Education. After her internships she decided teaching was more in line with her personality. She worked at the Andover School of Montessori and at Knowledge Beginnings in Andover. At a hockey game during her freshman year at Merrimack, she met a fellow student named Jason Lanziero from North Haven, Connecticut. They began dating in the fall. He was a good kid and we liked him a lot. His parents were divorced, so he mostly lived with his maternal grandparents, Rose and Neil. They were a little Italian couple who had been married over sixty years. They loved Jason dearly and gave him a great home and taught him to be respectful and kind.

Kenny and I both loved surprises. As Kenny's 50th birthday approached, I enlisted the help of the kids to concoct a great surprise gift for him. We had owned two small, old snowmobiles for years. We never went far on them because they always broke down and constantly needed parts and repairs. Kenny kept fixing them, but they weren't worth the time, effort, or expense.

He and I had window-shopped at the Polaris dealership in Arlington, with an eye to upgrade soon to new snowmobiles. So, the kids and I returned to make a deal. He had admired two of them, a blue double-seater for him and a red one for me. Eric, Monica, and I ordered them, along with a large trailer, and scheduled a delivery date.

On the Saturday before his birthday, he worked overtime at Polaroid in the morning. The trailer with the beautiful new snowmobiles arrived about 10:00 a.m. and the kids and their friends gathered in the back yard to watch the fun. Kenny came home about noon and parked his Tahoe in front of his right-side garage. When he came into the house, I asked him to come downstairs; I had something to show him. And there in the back yard sat the snowmobiles, on their trailer, glistening like jewels in the sun.

Kenny was floored. The kids all shouted, "Surprise!" and sang "Happy Birthday." He couldn't believe that I had pulled off this stunt behind his back. He deserved it, though. He always worked so hard to provide us with whatever we needed and wanted. We bought helmets and snowmobile suits and we were off.

He loved being out in nature and we spent several years snowmobiling in New Hampshire. On weekends we explored trails across gorgeous snow-covered terrain. We all enjoyed these weekend getaways and made these special memories together. I liked it much better than downhill skiing, which we used to do with the kids before my arthritic knees flared up.

Kenny always loved to try new things, especially related to cars. He had found out that the Loudon Speedway in New Hampshire was hosting a demolition derby. He bought a car at a used lot for cheap money. Eric and his friend, John, painted it black and orange, the colors of the Woburn Tanners. They took out the windows and painted the number "22" in white as its identification number. He borrowed a flatbed truck and off we went with family and friends, carrying signs and posters to cheer him on. Out he came screeching on the track with a smile on his face and thumbs up. He was rear-ended, which forced his windshield wipers to stay on. *Crash! Bang! Boom!* In terror, I shook like a leaf. He emerged into the finals, grinning like the Cheshire Cat. What a night that was! Life with Kenny was never boring and he was always shoving me out of my comfort zone.

Demolition Derby Car

Since we had given Eric and Monica huge high-school graduation parties, we decided to take them on a family vacation to celebrate their college commencements. The eight of us (Kenny, Linda, Auntie, Uncle, Eric, Karen, Monica, and Jason) went to Disney World for Eric and Karen's college celebration in the summer. Although it was hot and humid the lines were not too long and Fast Pass helped. We hit all of the theme parks and water parks and did our share of eating out. We danced at a few clubs and saw a comedy show. Kenny fulfilled another one of his dreams by riding in an Indy race car. He suited up and put his helmet on and with a big smile and a thumbs up rode in the pacer car. It went about two hundred miles an hour, which was his quickest speed ever and he loved every minute of it.

Two years later we all took a cruise from Boston to Bermuda for Monica and Jason's graduation from Merrimack College. We saw shows, gambled, and sunned and beach-combed. We would have had a better time on the beach had the Atlantic waters not been so choppy. But both were great trips and we all enjoyed spending time together.

Kenny in Disney pace car

During their senior year at Wentworth, Eric and Karen got engaged. After receiving their diplomas, they bought a condo together and married a year later. Kenny had reunited with Mike, a high-school friend and fellow car enthusiast. Mike was also a photographer and he graciously offered to capture the memories of Eric and Karen's wedding. Next came

Monica and Jason, whom we called Jay, who also got engaged in their senior year. They married the following year as well. This meant a flurry of college graduations, bridal showers, and weddings. Then came the best part—baby showers!

By now both of our kids were out of college and self-sufficient, and had their own homes, with minimal student debt. Kenny and I were alone in the house. We decided to renovate the downstairs into an in-law apartment downstairs for Auntie and Uncle.

I had been estranged from my mother and brother for many years. Auntie Lorraine and Uncle Bob still lived on the second floor of the two-family duplex in Somerville, with my mother on the first floor. Auntie had developed her own share of medical problems, and Uncle Bob, recovering from back surgery, could no longer climb the stairs to their second-floor apartment. Auntie and Uncle had a choice: either have Mom buy them out or convert the house into a condominium, so they could sell their half. Mom did not agree with either option. It boiled down to Auntie and Uncle converting the apartments into condo units at their own expense so they could move out. Because they were like parents to us and like grandparents to our kids, we asked them to come live with us.

We had no qualms about opening our house to them, because we had always got along well. As it was, I was their health-care proxy, so it would be much easier for me if they were under the same roof. They spent winters at their condo in Florida, so we did the renovations in the winter of 2005 while they were away. They picked out everything (furniture, appliances, and colors) before heading south.

Eric and Karen designed the space. Kenny sacrificed one of his garages in the back to renovate into a bedroom. We enlarged the bathroom and made it handicap-accessible. Our family room became their living room. It came out great and they were thrilled with it.

On the day of their return, the four kids (Eric, Karen, Monica and Jay) were there to welcome them into their new home. Eric and Karen had an even bigger surprise. They gave Kenny and me a jar of baby food to open, hinting that they were expecting their first child. We were going to be grandparents! The surprise doubled months later when they found out it was twin boys! Yahoo! We couldn't believe it. At Winchester Hospital on October 10th, nine weeks premature, Drew Kenneth and Jack Robert arrived. We were so happy!

We were scared, too. Jack was born with a laryngeal cleft tracheoesophageal fistula and was rushed in an ambulance to Boston. The emergency five-hour surgery at Children's Hospital reconnected his esophagus. Drew remained at Winchester learning to suck and breathe on his own, while Jack had to stay at Children's for some time. Eventually when Jack was stable and off the ventilator, he was brought back to Winchester. The twins bonded together briefly, but Jack had sleep apnea and had to be on a monitor. Drew was released, but Jack couldn't come home until a few months later.

It was a rough way for Eric and Karen to become new parents. They slept on hospital cots and changed into work clothes in Jack's hospital room. Both boys had lots of medical issues, but they both progressed amazingly well.

With the babies' arrival, Eric and Karen had outgrown their condo. They bought a four-bedroom ranch in Tewksbury, a fixer-upper, so we all pitched in to finish all kinds of projects, especially Kenny. Throughout the years, they renovated both inside and outside into a lovely home.

Shortly thereafter Monica and Jay announced they were expecting. In September, eleven months after the birth of the twins, we were blessed with Emma Rose's arrival. They were now living in Haverhill, Mass., in a colonial they bought. Three grandkids under a year—it was great! Eric got his sons and Monica got her daughter.

A few years later Cameron Jay was born to Monica and Jay, and nine months later Molly Grace was born to Eric and Karen. We now had five beautiful grandkids, the brunette Rennells and the curly-blonde Lanzieros.

Kenny and I loved being Nonna and Papa. It was rewarding to see our kids with their own children. They were all so handsome and beautiful! Being grandparents was everything they said it was and more. We were so lucky to see them all regularly and get to know them. All were unique with different temperaments and personalities. We loved them all so much.

Kenny had worked for Polaroid for twenty-eight years as a machine operator and then a maintenance man. In the past few years this huge corporation had become too complacent and did not advance with the new technology. Instant photos could no longer compete with digital cameras, which were becoming more popular. Once the layoffs began, rumor had it that the corporation was headed for bankruptcy. It was hard to believe. He loved his job, his hours, and his coworkers, and he had great medical benefits. But the situation indicated that it was time to look for another job.

When Polaroid finally closed, Kenny lost all of his stocks and pension, but I assured him that we would be fine. WOW was doing well. As he was getting older, I wanted him to work locally and enjoy his work.

Kenny didn't have a resume so Eric helped him create one. With only one full-time job on it, he looked either loyal or unmotivated. We hoped he would be seen as the former.

He applied to Brooksby Village, a fairly new retirement community in Peabody, owned and operated by Erickson Communities. The human resources department liked his years of experience and hired him immediately to take charge of the maintenance crew for the new assisted-living building called the Renaissance and a future skilled-care unit under construction. Kenny had his own office and a few guys under him. The job came with a big cut in pay, but he was still young enough to give them twenty years. He'd also be able to continue building his 401k and Social Security.

The campus was ninety acres of nicely manicured grounds, with all the modern amenities for its retirees. Some of the seniors had various kinds of dementia and were wary of new people. But Kenny soon became a familiar face, sitting with residents for breakfast and lunch and interacting with them. He was often found at bingo, woodworking, arts and crafts, rehab exercise time, or sitting out on the terrace with his elderly friends. Brooksby Village was family-oriented and he enjoyed working there. At dinner we'd swap stories, mine about the three-year-olds and his about the eighty-three-year-olds. A lot of our tales were similar, just at opposite ends of the age spectrum.

As a family, we were thrilled that none of the grandkids had to go to daycare. I had cribs and high chairs in my office a few days a week. At 12:30 I would take the older ones home for naps and to hang with me. Auntie and Uncle would watch one or all of the kids for a short period of time while I ran a few errands. Afternoons were filled with reading, arts and crafts, games, snacks, and pure joy. These youngsters' eyes lit up when Kenny came home from work. He always did projects with them and took them out to his garage. Often Uncle played with them in the yard while I prepared supper. They were bathed and in their pajamas by the time their parents arrived.

When we took them out, people always thought that the three older ones (Drew, Jack and Emma) were triplets. Cam and Molly were still toddlers. Drew and Jack were always calm and Emma, a little drama queen, was very chatty. To this day they have the same dispositions.

WOW was doing very well but Woburn Public Schools were rebuilding their elementary schools. This affected World of Wonder's enrollment significantly. The new facilities had extra square-footage to house preschool and inclusion classes. Students on an individual education plan could go for free with their siblings at a discounted rate. Parents with an older child in elementary school could drop off their preschooler at the same building, where they often qualified for the free breakfast program. It was difficult to compete with this, and it forced us to downsize.

We eliminated our afternoon sessions. As the owner of a small business, I quickly learned we need to have a Plan B up my sleeve for when Plan A failed. You have to reinvent yourself depending upon the need, in order to stay fiscally sound. Thankfully most of our clientele were professional people who could afford a private school to give their child the best early childhood experience in a small, controlled environment. But a percentage of families had to do what was cost-effective for them and their individual child. We modified the center and things were still going well. I loved my job and loved going to work every day. I was grateful to be home on snow days, school vacations, and summers with my own kids. I was thrilled to be available now to babysit my grandchildren. It was ideal for me and my staff, who had younger children of their own.

It was great to watch our grandchildren develop. Soon our three older ones were deep into extracurricular activities (soccer and T-ball). In soccer, no one knew the difference between offense and defense, and in T-ball, everyone ran around in the outfield when the ball was finally hit. Hardly anyone could find the bases. They were all so innocent and adorable. We looked forward to their weekly games.

We babysat Cameron and Molly and they loved to play together with puzzles and blocks. Once they were age-appropriate, they came to WOW with me, while their older siblings were in school full-time. Cameron was a curious and active little boy and Molly was more cautious whose dimpled smile could light up a room. They were all unique and Kenny and I loved them each for who they were and we were thrilled to spend time with them.

In 1986, Kenny and I had bought into a timeshare in Mashpee on Cape Cod. When the kids were young, we often exchanged it to visit other resorts in various states. Then with the grandchildren, the entire family always spent the third week of July at Sea Mist. It was a horseshoe-shaped cluster of condos and townhouses with a centrally located clubhouse in a rustic setting. The mature trees and open grassy areas provided a variety of shade and sun. Everyone enjoyed the outdoor and indoor pools, mini-golf, shuffleboard, and ping-pong. We made many family memories there and still enjoy going today. One of our annual traditions has been for Kenny and me to walk the five grandkids to a nearby Dunkin Donuts, then take a photo of the younger generation on our favorite bench. I would shop with them for new backpacks, and later, Kenny would take them on a hike while their parents slept in.

Our Grandkids at Cape Cod

One of the time-share exchanges was in Las Vegas. We took a long weekend in the fall. Kenny and I loved the entertainment there, including roulette. On one trip, we noticed that the hotel's in-ground hot tub had no heat, just jets. I thought this would be an ideal summer asset for our backyard. I brought it up to Kenny, but he wanted to think about it before going ahead on the project. He researched it and we installed a ten-person hot tub. It looked like a small in-ground pool. The first summer we loved it.

The pool company advised us to empty the water in the fall, to winterize it. When Kenny uncovered the hot tub the next spring, however, he discovered that frost heaves had tipped the spa, damaging the hoses, which were brittle. We had been too ignorant to take into account the drastic differences in weather conditions between the southwest and northeast. The spa had to be hoisted out of the ground, and Kenny and Eric spent endless hours in the yard, re-digging the entire pit.

At the time, Boston (thirty miles south of us) was in the middle of the so-called Big Dig construction project. Our next-door neighbor would come out on his deck to monitor our progress on the spa. He called it The Little Dig.

For two years, he shed blood, sweat, tears, and cash to make it functional again. I had to admit that this was the worst idea I ever had. It pissed off Kenny. What a disaster!

His friend Mike reintroduced him to Roger, who had graduated from Tewksbury High with them. He, too, had a passion for cars and we went to several car shows with him and his girlfriend, Yvonne.

In one of the want-ad catalogs, Kenny and Roger spotted a barn find in New Hampshire. (I had never heard the term but learned that it was an old deserted car that had sat in a barn, unattended for years.) Kenny and Roger went after it. Kenny drove his Tahoe with the trailer hitch and in the pouring rain, they towed the treasure to Roger's house. They had a blast.

It was now 2009. Retirement approached steadily, and we could see it coming, down the road. The kids were financially independent and everyone was happy.

Kenny's gall bladder flared up and he had surgery to remove it. Even after that, his liver readings were elevated, indicating that something wasn't quite right about his health. It troubled us a little, but we weren't overly concerned.

We spent our thirty-fifth wedding anniversary in Aruba. The Caribbean weather was always sunny and we spent endless days at the beach drinking pina coladas, and dined every night at different ethnic restaurants.

When we came home Kenny developed a problem with his knee. It was always sore. X-rays and MRIs showed that he had torn his meniscus, although we didn't know how he had done that. He had day surgery in December, then was doing fine after a brief rehab.

Near the end of January 2010, the kids and grandkids had caught the flu. Kenny came home from work one day feeling nauseous and had stomach cramps. We assumed he had caught the kids' stomach bug. He complained about irregular bowel movements. He was fifty-seven years old. At that age, irregularity is not uncommon. He stayed home from work for a few days, but didn't feel better. Then one night he had severe stomach pain and vomited constantly vomiting. No longer was he was throwing up food; it was dark-colored bile. Nothing we tried to ease his discomfort worked, neither ginger ale nor broth. When I saw him hung over the toilet, moaning in pain, I knew it was time to go to the hospital.

I wanted to call an ambulance but he insisted that I take him in my car. It was a chore to get him dressed, even in simple sweat pants. Off to Winchester Hospital we went with a puke bucket at hand. Although it was only a few miles' drive, it was an awful bumpy ride and it seemed like an eternity to get there. I pulled up to the Emergency Room entrance and ran in to get him a wheelchair. By that time, he couldn't even walk because the pain was so excruciating. Once I saw how the nurses and doctors assisted him, I broke into tears, relieved for the help. After a few minutes I collected myself and went into the hospital room with him.

I had never seen him like that, not in all the years we had been together. They whisked us into a curtained room. The pain and vomiting worsened. They gave him an IV of pain medications, which barely touched him. I don't know how but they did a CT scan, which revealed a bowel obstruction. The doctors explained that the bowel had a kink, like a garden hose. He needed to have a nasal gastric tube put in to drain the bile from his stomach to relieve his pain. Supposedly this usually repairs the damaged section. I had no idea what that was or how awful it was to put in.

I trembled as I stood alone outside of his little room. A nice nurse knew what was going on and stayed with me to reassure me. I saw a doctor and a nurse go into his room with plastic bibs and lots of tubing. Then I heard Kenny scream like he was being stabbed. Finally, there was silence and I was permitted to see him. A tube, taped to his nose, came out of his nostril, draining blackish fluid into a plastic bottle. I never saw anything like it. It was horrible, but at least his pain had diminished.

Terrified at what this might all mean, I held Kenny's hand, hoping to comfort him as well as myself. The doctor promised that the tube was not permanent, that the kink would repair itself, and he would be fine. I asked how to prevent this from happening again and he said it was highly unlikely, that this instance was a fluke. I wanted to believe him, but after what I witnessed, I had my doubts. I stayed with Kenny all night in the emergency room. By morning, a bed became available and they admitted him. I called the kids in the morning to tell them what had transpired. Auntie and Uncle were in Florida, so the kids provided moral support.

He stayed in the hospital for a few days with the gastrointestinal tube then they clamped it since it was hardly draining. Eventually they introduced soft, bland foods like broth and Jell-O that he could tolerate without throwing up. They did another Xray and the kink in the bowel had improved. Out came the tube and he was discharged. He stayed home from work for a few days. He was still feeling sluggish and his eating was sporadic. He tried to go back to work but still was weak and nauseous.

A week later was Valentine's Day. Annually we always went out to dinner with our friends, Bil and Terry. I told Kenny we should not go, but I think he did not want to disappoint me, since I always loved the romance of Valentine's Day. We went into Newbury Street in Boston and he barely ate. He spent most of the time going back and forth to the bathroom. He was very quiet and not his jovial self, which worried all of us. Bil and Terry dropped us off at home about ten o'clock. Within an hour, Kenny was slumped on the bathroom floor, throwing up that black bile again. This time I called an ambulance because he hadn't the strength to get up off the floor. We left the house in total disarray—it was a debacle.

The ambulance hit every pot hole, and Kenny screamed in pain at each one. The paramedics called ahead for a stretcher and rushed him into the emergency room again. While we waited there, Kenny checked the time on the clock on the wall. It was almost midnight on February 13th and when it read 12:00 a.m. he croaked out "Happy Valentine's Day" with a weak smile. He knew that it was one of my favorite holidays. Leave it to Kenny to think of me amidst this horror show.

Once again, he had a CT scan, revealing another bowel blockage, and they installed another horrible NG tube. This was becoming a pattern, not a fluke. Black bile filled bottle after bottle, and it took longer to relieve the abdominal pain. Clearly, he could not continue this way. I sat on two chairs outside his room all night long and dozed. He had a roommate, so I couldn't stay in the room. I had gone in the ambulance with him so I had no car. I didn't want to call the kids in the middle of the night and worry them.

Needless to say, it was not a Happy Valentine's Day. When the kids came the next day, we met with a new doctor and he reviewed all of Kenny's medical records. Not even a polyp showed up from his colonoscopy six months before. The doctor was puzzled and ordered another CT scan, using contrast. It was hard enough to swallow that pasty white stuff, but it was beyond brutal to do it with an NG tube down his throat. It was so frustrating and upsetting to watch Kenny suffer so much.

The doctor called in specialists to determine if it was ulcerative colitis or Crohn's disease, neither of which we knew anything about. Little did we know that either of those horrible-sounding diagnoses would have been a blessing. I went home to shower and pack an overnight bag. Eric and Monica stayed with him, because he didn't have strength enough to press the call-button for the nurse.

The next day, February 15th, was President's Day, and the hospital had no scheduled surgeries, so the doctor booked an operating room so he could go in laparoscopically to see what was going on. He said it would take about two hours. The exploratory operation was scheduled for noon.

Because of the holiday, everyone was home from work and school. The surgeon said his associate would be assisting him for a second opinion. The associate was the head of the GI department, and she had years of experience. Strangely, I found that both comforting and nerve-wracking.

I told the kids to stay home with their families in the morning, but to meet me in the hospital family waiting room about 1:30 p.m. to hear what the doctor had to say when he finished the inspection.

I sat in that dreaded room alone trying to read a magazine and staring at the landscape artwork on the white walls. After about forty-five minutes the surgeons came out. I wondered how they had finished so quickly. That was never a good sign. The assistant surgeon pulled no punches. She said that they had found a malignant tumor in his small bowel, already metastasized to the wall and lining of the bowel. They removed it and resected his bowel, but were not able to clear the margins. It was Stage 4 cancer.

The doctor had done this kind of operation many times before; her explanation was robotic. She had no bedside manner and expressed not an ounce of compassion. Kenny's humanity didn't matter; he was just another patient.

Not to us, he wasn't! He was my husband, the father of my children, and a grandfather of five. This horrible news hit me like a two-by-four. By the time the kids got there, I was in a near-faint. The two doctors returned to explain this devastating news to us in greater detail. The surgery was a tough one; Kenny came out of it with a ten-inch incision down his chest. I asked them when we should tell him about the cancer. They advised waiting until the next day. Right now, he was heavily sedated for the pain, and he'd be in the recovery room for a while. The doctor said he would be in the next morning to talk with both of us.

This was an absolute nightmare! Eric, Monica, and I were a mess. Monica was hysterical. Eric stayed strong, although I could see how it challenged him. They let us see Kenny after about an hour. Eric came with me, but Monica couldn't deal with it, so a nurse stayed with her. In the recovery room, tubes were everywhere. Kenny was so heavily medicated that he could barely open his eyes. But when he saw us, he smiled. He croaked out, "I think they fixed the problem and I am fine." Nothing could have been further from the truth. The recovery room nurses must have reassured him that he was okay. I was in total panic mode and petrified of the unknown.

One of Monica's friends was the head nurse on Three South, so she managed to get Kenny into a private room. The kids came after work to see him, and we decided to not to inform anyone else about the cancer until Kenny knew what he was facing. Everyone scared for him. I stayed on a recliner with him that night, and it was rough. He moaned a lot, and I pressed his call-button at least once every hour, for another infusion of pain medication.

The nurses informed me that his bowel would reawaken in a day or so. The next day, Tuesday the 16th, was gloomy, with off-and-on snow. I arrived early in the morning, and Kenny and I waited for the doctor to come and for his bowel to wake up.

The bowel woke up first. This kind of surgery shuts it down, and reawakening means raging diarrhea. It poured out of him. He was hooked up to IV fluids, but they couldn't keep up with the discharge, and he became weaker and more dehydrated by the minute.

By six o'clock in the evening, the kids arrived from work, but the doctor still hadn't. Kenny still had no explanation about his condition. By 6:30 we decided to tell Kenny ourselves, but just then the doctor joined us. He was very matter-of-fact, knowing what we had all been through in the last two days. He explained that the colonoscopy had not revealed the tumor because it only looks at the large intestine. The small intestine can only be viewed surgically. This small-bowel cancer was very rare; only about one hundred people in the United States had been diagnosed with it.

When Kenny was told how courageous he was, he asked how soon before he could start a treatment plan. The surgeon said he could have chemo there at Winchester Cancer Center, and that he would send an oncologist tomorrow to discuss options with us.

Now we had to inform our family and friends about his cancer. First Auntie and Uncle who loved Kenny like a son. They were devastated and flew home from Florida immediately. Lorraine and Lee were in disbelief. All of our cousins and friends were more than dismayed. All the special people in our lives had the same reaction—shocked. They all rallied around us with phone calls and kind words. This would take a village!

I finally went home, alone for the first time. Auntie and Uncle were back from Florida and had cleaned up the bathroom and kitchen for me. I walked upstairs to our kitchen alone with a void and emptiness in my heart. Our once warm and cozy house seemed so cold and rigid. I had held back my tears for days. Finally, I had an opportunity to cry and unwind. I took a bubble bath and sat in the tub with this very eerie feeling of the possibility of living at 6 Sheila Avenue without Kenny. I regrouped the best I could, packed a bag, and went back to the hospital to relieve Eric.

In the few hours while I was away, Kenny took a turn for the worst. His blood pressure plunged and his bowel woke up on overload. He was too weak to sit up in the chair and we feared he would not make it through the day.

As a family we all discussed Kenny's prognosis and were all thinking the same thing. This was so unusual and serious that we should get a second opinion in Boston. No hospital wanted to take on a patient with stage 4 cancer who had already had surgery at a small local hospital, but the Rennells joined forces to transfer him. Medical insurance coverage was also an issue. We all started making contacts with anyone and everyone we knew in the medical field. Everyone recommended Dana Farber. Patients came from all over the world for cancer treatment there, so this became our mission.

A local oncologist was sent to us for a consult. We quickly got the impression that this situation was out of her league. She concurred that a Boston hospital would be his best bet.

My daughter-in-law, Karen, knew an oncology nurse at Dana Farber, who arranged for a consultation with a GI oncologist in a few weeks. After about two weeks at Winchester Hospital Kenny was finally discharged but was very sore and wobbly. He found great comfort in being home, though.

We were both petrified but did our best to be optimistic.

It was school vacation week and I had to catch up on my work at World of Wonder. I had not done mail or the payroll or cleaned bathrooms. Our second home was 905 Main Street, so when I put that key in the door, I ran into my office, sat at my desk, and cried and cried, out of control. I couldn't imagine being here without Kenny. It was a huge reality check for me about how uncertain our future was.

My office was full of family photos. The one that resonated with me was of the four of us in 1987 when we opened the school. In that one, Kenny and I are in our mid-thirties, Eric is eight, and Monica six. Our faces are full of optimism about our new venture.

For years these photos motivated me. Now, they broke my heart.

The Rennell Family in 1987

Joan, Terry, and Denise were not only my administrative team at WOW but also close friends. I had to tell them Kenny's grim diagnosis in person. All three came to my house and reassured me that they could hold down the fort at WOW. My main job now was as Kenny's caregiver. We tried not to do research on the computer but we were all guilty of it. We learned that "terminal" and "stage 4" were usually synonymous and the mortality rate was six months to two years. Oh my God, was he in big trouble.

As Kenny recovered at home, we both had to learn how differently his body reacted to food and drink now. It was downright scary. He struggled to build up strength so he could start chemotherapy as soon as possible. Physically he was doing the best he could. Mentally I was taking one day at a time, but the fear of the unknown was killing me. Winging it was definitely not my forte.

Eric and Monica came with us to the consultation with the GI oncologist. as an extra pair of ears. My poor kids were so upset to see their dad like this and facing this journey ahead. They were so compassionate to both of us. I felt helpless, so caught up in my own grief that I could not fix my kids' hurt. I felt like I couldn't be there to babysit the grandkids, to support my own kids, and I was grateful that they had each other for support. Kenny was now my top priority. Part of me was ridden with guilt over that, but part of me knew that's what I had to do. My five grandkids always gave me such joy, but it frightened me that nothing and no one brought me happiness anymore.

We all sat in the oncologist's office at Dana Farber, a white, sterile room with lots of diplomas in custom frames hanging on the walls. Our new doctor was a young Harvard graduate with tons of knowledge but with no personality at all. He reviewed scans with us, barely looked up from his laptop, and showered us with tons of medical terminology. It never sat right with me when he told us that in his career that he only had one other patient with advanced small-bowel cancer. There was no one else presently being treated at Dana Farber for this rare cancer.

He gave us the statistics that there were only one hundred other people in the country with this disease. When I asked him, "Where are the other ninety-nine?" he answered unsympathetically he did not know. We had anticipated meeting other families going through the same thing for moral support, but clearly this was not the case. It was disheartening to realize how alone we were.

Because the doctor didn't have a chemo strategy specific for this rare cancer, he planned to treat it like colon cancer. He arranged to install a port in Kenny's chest the next week, where he would receive the infusions, a strong regimen that would make Kenny tired and sick. Anti-nausea medication would help, and Kenny would come home with a chemo pump, active for another forty-eight hours. He could either come back to the hospital to have it disconnected or we could do it at home ourselves. Kenny decided to disconnect it at home. We learned about the tubing and flushing, which saved trips into Boston. That proved a much-needed break for both of us.

They gave us a tour of the chemo wing. While a poisonous fluid flushed their veins, patients pretended to be normal while watching TV, reading, working on laptops. Volunteers with cheery smiles pushed food carts and book trays around.

The dual port (to access either side in case one got blocked) was implanted in the upper right side of his chest. Poor Kenny was still recovering from the surgery his body had just endured. We were set up for Fridays every other week so he could unhook on Sunday and rest on Monday. If he felt well enough, he'd go to work on Tuesday. The doctor thought initially Kenny might be able to still work, depending upon the chemo's side effects. The schedule was grueling.

We took the kids out to the 99 Restaurant in Stoneham to celebrate that chemo was an option for him. We toasted the fact that we had a plan and to hope for a miracle. Kenny said he was glad it was him with the cancer and not one of us or the grandkids. He reassured us that if there was anyone that could do this, it was him. Here he was, comforting us, while he battled for his life.

We were crazily thankful that there was a plan. So far, no one had said that the case was hopeless. Eric was emotional on the inside but put on a brave front for us. Our daughter-in-law Karen was especially good for Eric because he was comfortable venting his frustration to her. She was level-headed and she kept things in perspective for him. Our son-in-law Jay, on the other hand, had a difficult time comforting Monica.

While Kenny had been at Winchester Hospital, we were advised to attend a Cancer Support Group. I wanted to go but Kenny did not. He didn't want to talk to strangers about his private life. I went alone the first time and Eric came with me the second time. Everyone was great and were just like us, trying to figure this out. Lee told Kenny that he was being selfish, that he ought to go for my sake, if not his own. That was the first time these friends had ever disagreed strongly and exchanged harsh words.

Kenny eventually came to the group with me and he admitted it helped both of us. His story encouraged other people and he became a valuable member of the group. We made new friends who were in the same boat. The old phrase, "misery loves company," proved all too true. We continued to go for about three years. During this span of time, we learned to live with cancer as a chronic illness. The message was to do whatever you had to, to keep it dormant. Everyone fought like hell for every extra day.

We found out that the daffodil was the cancer survivor flower. In the spring they were plentiful, so I filled our house with both fresh and artificial ones. We even bought a huge silk daffodil floor plant that we placed behind our headboard to surround him with healing power. Cancer pamphlets came and went, explaining how to prepare for the side effects of chemo. Nothing could have prepared us for the reality of the experience for either patient or caregiver.

I went to work while he relaxed at home. Auntie and Uncle checked on him several times a day. They were wonderful to us. They made sure he ate and drank. They spent time chatting with him until I got home at about 1:00 p.m. They did errands and cooked meals to lighten our burden.

My staff at work rallied around us, big time. They prepared meals, sent flowers and plants, and most importantly, ran the preschool as best they could without me. My secretary/bookkeeper Joan was my rock, hard-working and conscientious. Trustworthy Joan collected tuition and paid bills. Her sense of humor always made the office a fun place. I gave consent for her and Monica to sign the ADP payroll checks. My assistant directors really stepped things up and took over the reins for me while managing their own classrooms. My nurse, Mary, always shared her expertise. She was my medical informant and helped me to understand the terminology. Some days, she even volunteered to sit with Kenny while I worked. Her husband, Dave, was now retired, so he offered to snowplow, shovel, and sand the walkways during bad weather. We so appreciated it and it was one less thing for us to worry about.

Monica did everything I used to do behind the scenes. She cleaned the parking lot, kept the playground intact, washed the windows, vacuumed, and took out the trash. We owned the building and as landlords, we were responsible to our upstairs tenant, so my son-in-law, Jay, and my son, Eric, took over the cleaning and general maintenance upstairs. They were so helpful. Kenny's mind was relieved knowing the boys were taking care of it.

In the middle of all this chaos, I tried the best I could to shield Kenny from our financial situation. I was self-employed, so he had always carried the medical insurance through his job. My days were spent applying for short-term disability, talking back and forth with human resources at Brooksby Village (who were amazing through all of this), and calculating his sick time and vacation time. All of the typical bill paying, errands, cooking, housekeeping, and food shopping seemed insurmountable.

Knowledge is power. We read all the pamphlets and information mailed to us, cover to cover. We were both absolutely terrified about this treatment plan. Soon it was March 17th, Saint Patrick's Day, Kenny's first day of chemotherapy. Every visit there involved three appointments. First were the vitals, weigh-in, blood work, and port flush. Next, we met with the oncologist to discuss the results and to order the next chemo regimen. Last was the infusion.

At 8:00 a.m., we entered the GI Cancer wing dressed in Irish green shirts, trying to portray a positive energy we did not feel. Sallow patients waited there. Their knowing expressions confirmed that we were rookies. The receptionist was a miserable older lady who barely looked up when Kenny stated his name. She gave him an identification wrist bracelet, the first of hundreds he would ultimately wear. Then we sat and waited to be called. A serious young nurse came out and called for "Kenneth R." (We soon learned that for confidentiality, they never called out last names.) She never said good morning or asked how we were. She just followed her daily routine.

I was always quite organized. I had brought a notebook to record the date, Kenny's weight, and his blood pressure results. When the young nurse finished with Kenny, she escorted us to the port room. A much nicer middle-aged nurse greeted us. She gave us her name and explained the process while she drew Kenny's blood.

Then into the oncologist's office we went. With his face still in his computer, he explained the names of the chemo solutions in Kenny's regimen, clinically, like a robot. He scheduled us for the next visit in two weeks, then sent us off to the infusion room.

The infusion room was furnished with recliners in which patients sat, each strung up to an array of plastic bags of fluids, some white, some clear, each bag draining into a tube connected to the patient's port. After seeing that, it wasn't as easy to smile cheerfully at the other patients. A pleasant nurse escorted us to a recliner. She gave me a chair, too, for me to sit with Kenny. An assortment of books and magazines was available to make the time go by more pleasantly, as well as a TV.

By now it was noon and the nurse had yet to begin Kenny's treatment. The nurse gave him an anti-nausea medicine, then the chemo began. The staff walked around with cold drinks and lunches, and showed me a little kitchen where I could make coffee or tea and grab bite-sized snacks. Kenny couldn't swallow anything except ginger ale.

About an hour into it, with the smell of the plastic tubes and the sensation of the chemo through his veins, Kenny began to dry-heave. Poor thing: it was brutal. The nurse assured us this was normal. It sure didn't look normal to us. He finally finished his second bag of fluid. They showed him how to connect and disconnect his pump. I was thankful that Kenny felt confident enough to do this. They left us with instructions and gave us his prescriptions. I went to the pharmacy loaded up with all we needed and put them into a tiny blue hospital canvas bag. I would soon grow to hate the very sight of that bag.

Kenny handed me the car keys, a novelty for both of us, and we headed home, laden with that little pink puke container and boxes of tissues. We made our way down Storrow Drive, picked up I-93, and then took Route 128. Home again, in our blessed sanctuary!

Once we found a rhythm to Kenny's chemo routine in Boston, we would call Lee when Kenny's treatment was done. Lee worked for the commuter rail, and we passed the massive purple building that served as a maintenance garage for the MBTA. After our call, he would stand in the huge, open garage bay and wave to us. It comforted us greatly to see his smiling face. We both knew how awful he felt about his best buddy's ordeal.

Back home, Kenny went directly to bed. I lay beside him until we both fell asleep to the swish of the chemo through the pump. I had worried that this constant chemo reminder would keep us from sleeping, but it became "white noise," a background noise that could be soothing, in a sense.

Best friend Lee with Kenny

By Sunday, at a certain time, the pump was programmed to beep when it had run its forty-eight-hour course. It was ready to be unplugged. After the disconnect Kenny was so exhausted that he went straight to bed and slept until the next morning. Through the night I would wake him up as scheduled for his steroid medicine and water. My new routine included packing the pump in the provided UPS box and dropping it off at the store for shipping back to the hospital.

Our kitchen table resembled a science lab, constantly covered with a sanitized blue cloth, which was invisible under the profusion of syringes, flushes, and tubing. The TV tray beside the bed resembled a mini-pharmacy.

Kenny was determined to go to back to work, and struggled mightily to do so on that first Tuesday. That was a tough day, but over the next few days, little by little, he felt better. Before we knew it, though, two weeks had passed and his next treatment was due. No sooner would he feel better than it was time for another round of chemo. It was a vicious cycle!

One Sunday about noon, while he waited for the pump to beep, he decided to spend the remaining hour downstairs in the garage, tinkering with his Hot Rod. Soon he came back upstairs to where I was in the kitchen. He said there was a problem. There sure was! His shirt was full of blood. The tube had disconnected too early. He was his usual calm self, but it scared both of us. I reported it to the doctor, then rushed Kenny to the hospital. They were waiting for him and we spent the whole day there.

This was our schedule for several months, until his doctor ordered the next CT scans. They showed no further spreading of the cancer cells, but no improvement, either. The oncologist seemed pleased, but I was not. I got to thinking that he put Kenny through all of this just to keep things the same. Quickly we realized that with his type of cancer, the goal was to prevent it from metastasizing more, and that success was considered keeping it at bay. The cancer would probably never leave; we aimed to keep it dormant.

The Brooksby people at Kenny's job were fabulous. Since he was still able to work a few days a week, he was still on the payroll. This meant we still had benefits, which we desperately needed.

When we got the bill for his chemotherapy, we almost fell over. It cost $22,000 each time he went. We had no idea how expensive this would get, and to spend almost $50,000 a month to be sick and suffer was a disgrace. But at this point we had no other choice. We both liked to have a plan and be in control of our lives. Now we floundered helplessly. Now we knew, first-hand, that cancer is a multi-million-dollar industry. This was why we were at a new high-tech facility in Boston.

Kenny had to take powerful narcotics three times a day to manage the bowel movements. Several times we went back and forth to the hospital for IV fluids, since he was constantly dehydrated. This type of GI chemo did not cause hair loss, and at first Kenny looked fine, but he became thinner and more frail as time passed. It took a serious toll on his body, but he stayed mentally strong and fought bravely through it all. He was a trooper!

After four months of treatment, the doctor said that since the cancer had not spread, Kenny's best chance at extending his life was surgery.

This type of cancer was two-dimensional, not three-dimensional as most tumors are. It presented like grains of salt spread throughout the abdomen. The idea was to scrape the cells from his bowel. But the thought of the trauma that Kenny's body had already endured was scary.

With this in mind, we met with a wonderful GI surgeon from Brigham and Women's Hospital. She seemed confident and reassured us that he was lucky that surgery was an option, a viable alternative. After we discussed it, he decided it was worth the risk, so the surgeon scheduled him for the end of June, first thing in the morning. They gave him a two-week break from the chemo treatment, so he could gain strength prior to the operation.

We arrived at six a.m. The kids and Auntie and Uncle sat with me in the waiting room through the four-hour ordeal. We praying together and often went to sit in the chapel. Every hour, the liaison nurse updated us on his progress. It went according to schedule, which helped our anxiety. In a few hours they directed us to the family room.

The doctor finally came and explained how the operation went. She said Kenny did fine and the operation was a success. She had removed all the visible cells. Of course, there was no way to know if microscopic cells escaped to other parts of the body, but as of now he was cancer-free, labeled "NED," which stands for "no evidence detected at this time."

We were elated! This was our first bit of good news in a long time. As soon as they let me, I went in to see him, and as soon as he knew I was there, he opened his eyes. I told him the good news. For the first time ever, I saw a tear of relief run down his cheek. He winked at me.

Recuperation at the hospital resulted in more suffering, but Kenny made progress every day. We walked the halls overlooking the beautiful Boston skyline and watched the Fourth of July fireworks from The Esplanade. We were cautiously optimistic. Kenny was in a different mindset from before, which helped his physical recuperation.

Kenny was always a proud, self-sufficient guy who never wanted or needed help with anything. But through this journey, fear was obvious in his eyes. He had always taken care of all of us, so this reversal was hard for him. This was a huge adjustment for both of us. I had never seen him vulnerable before. Old Kenny would have insisted that I go home and eat, rest, and shower. New Kenny felt more secure and comfortable when I stayed with him.

That first day after the surgery, he asked the nurses, "Do you have a sheet, pillow and a cot for my wife? She is staying overnight with me." Thereafter we bunked down nightly, with my cot cuddled up to his bed, and fell asleep holding hands. Sometimes when neither of us could sleep, I crawled into bed with him and we held each other all night. That's how we always survived the tough times.

Boy! Did we ever want our old life back! Therapists and counselors insisted that we had to find a "new normal". Kenny would snort in disgust and say, "There's nothing normal about the life we're living now."

After a recovery period, Kenny returned to the two-week chemo routine. After this operation, going back to work was out of the question. He went on short-term disability, which turned into long-term disability. It was all he could do to function daily. He didn't even drive much anymore. For him to sit in the passenger seat (and being okay with it and not critiquing my driving skills) was a surreal experience for both of us. Instead of being frustrated about it, however, he conceded gracefully. Having someone else drive him around was the least of his problems.

We were cautiously hopeful for a while, until new CT scans showed new growth of cancer cells. A horrible turning point for us was when we had a consultation with both the oncologist and surgeon at Dana Farber. They said the chemo was no longer working. There was nothing else they could do for him and he should get his affairs in order. These were dreaded words we never wanted to hear.

We drove home in the car in silence. How were we going to tell the kids? What else could we do? What would happen next? We held it together until we got home, then we both cried. That was the first time

Kenny admitted he was scared. I had been frightened all along, but now I was totally terrified.

Kenny's family had a huge history of cancer, so I knew his sisters were frightened for him. Paula and Marsha were so helpful to me, kind to their brother, and such a great support system to us. They gave him massages when his body was so sore, did Reiki on him to promote healing, and spent lots of time hanging out with us. His sister Claudia came down from New Hampshire to visit him in the hospital and at home. Kenny's niece, Amanda, called often with words of encouragement. The Rennells are not quitters, and in a crisis, we never give up. We always rally and seek other options.

The bad news discouraged our kids, but they weren't ready to give up yet, either. Eric researched case histories of people with small-bowel cancer. He discovered a Mexican doctor named Jesus Esquivel, the guru of a new experimental surgery called HIPEC (hyperthermic intraperitoneal chemotherapy). Esquivel's method was to open up the abdomen and pour heated chemotherapy into the gut to kill the cancer cells. The process had recently been approved in this country. We initially thought it must be available in Boston since that's the hub of medical research. To our dismay, this surgeon practiced in a small hospital in Baltimore, Maryland, associated with John Hopkins. He had done several of these procedures with some success.

We called to find out what was required for acceptance. Monica and Eric helped me make contacts, and we gathered disks of all his previous scans to submit to Baltimore. Monica drove me in and out of Winchester and Boston, with her kids in the back seat, to gather all of his medical records. Eric arranged paperwork to be sent by certified mail. It seemed endless.

Kenny had to meet other criteria, too, before he would be considered a viable candidate. Other than the cancer, he was healthy and had no co-morbidities. He was fifty-eight years old. The cancer had not metastasized to any other vital organs.

By the grace of God, the doctor sent us a letter saying he would meet with us. He thought Kenny might be eligible for his HIPEC. Eric booked our flight.

The night before we headed to Maryland, Kenny and I had a heart-to-heart. He said he wanted to stay alive as long as he could to be with me, Eric and Monica and the grandkids. He knew that Drew, Jack and Emma had known him when he was healthy so he had done lots of fun things with them. He felt bad that Cameron and Molly were so young when he was diagnosed that they only knew him when he was sick on the couch. He wanted his grandkids to be old enough to remember good things about him.

The four of us took the commuter flight to Baltimore. As I saw everyone boarding the plane at Boston's Logan Airport, I kept thinking that the majority of them were happy and perhaps headed to a vacation destination. I wished we had the same to look forward to. We left Logan Airport at 6:00 a.m. on Jet Blue for a 10:00 a.m. consultation with Dr. Jesus Esquivel, MD, Oncology, Surgery—a doctor in whom we placed our last hope to save Kenny's life.

Fortunately, Kenny was feeling better for the flight. He was in between chemo treatments. It did worry us that we didn't know what was going on inside him without the chemo.

We rented a car to get to Ascension Saint Agnes Hospital, a small local facility in a deprived area specializing in several fields, including cancer treatment. The doctor's assistant, Robin, greeted all of us with a big smile and a welcoming attitude. A nurse practitioner examined Kenny, then she brought us into a small office, where once again, we waited to hear his fate.

A few minutes later Dr. Esquivel walked in. He was a handsome Mexican man in his forties who reminded us of Desi Arnaz from the *I Love Lucy* television show. He carried a big folder with all of Kenny's test results. After a little chit-chat, he got down to business. After reviewing everything, he thought Kenny was a good candidate for his surgery. He gave us a brief history of his experience with HIPEC and had some questions for us.

The most pertinent one proved to be, "Kenny, what happened to your appendix?"

Kenny replied, "I never had it out so I assume I still have it."

The doctor snickered and said, "No you don't. It's gone."

The four of us thought we heard him wrong. No one had ever mentioned Kenny's appendix before. *What the hell?*

Dr. Esquivel said he could not prove it, but his assumption was that Kenny's second bowel obstruction was not a blockage. He theorized that the original source of the malignant tumor was in the appendix and that the tumor had ruptured, with a piece of it ending up in the small bowel.

This information confused us even more. Appendix cancer was even rarer than small-bowel cancer.

Dr. Esquivel had a slot for surgery in early November. He kindly but bluntly explained that this was not a cure. But one of his patients was twelve years out from this surgery, and new medical techniques and advances came out every year.

He gave us time to discuss our decision in private. We were all in. It was the only chance Kenny had left and we were grateful for it. When Dr. Esquivel returned, we told him to book the surgery. He grinned pleasantly, pleased to be able to help.

Now that the HIPEC was the plan, the doctor explained the procedure in more detail. It would take about five hours. First, he would open Kenny up and clear away any of the cancer cells, which he described as a film-like substance. Then he would pump heated chemotherapy solution directly into the abdomen. Two nurses would massage the abdomen for a couple of hours by straddling his stomach, to swish the chemo around. Then he would close the abdomen.

He was straightforward about how tough this surgery was. He had done over one hundred of them. Some patients had to spend a few days in the ICU, then in the hospital a week or two, and heal a little close by, in Baltimore, before returning home. We could expect to spend a month or six weeks there. None of this intimidated Kenny; he was so brave. The doctor left the room with handshakes all around.

We received a brief tour of the hospital. It was small but nicely appointed, and everyone was friendly. That should not have mattered to me, but it did. This place would be our home away from home for a while.

The four of us went to the cafeteria for lunch. As we ate, the doctor walked through the room. Everyone who worked there knew him and he greeted everyone with a genuine smile. When he saw us there, he greeted us and asked if we had any other questions for him. That was so nice of him, and we could not get over how down-to-earth he was. When he left, several of the staff approached us and told us he was highly respected and that we were lucky to have him as our surgeon. That definitely put our minds at ease! We felt great comfort knowing that Dr. Esquivel was the one in whose hands we trusted Kenny's life.

Our flight home wasn't until 7:00 p.m., so we browsed around the inside and outside of the hospital. At the gift shop, I purchased a small statue of Saint Agnes, to whom I prayed for a successful result.

The hospital was right in the middle of a low-income area where homeless people slept on the sidewalks. Selfishly, I wondered: Where will I stay? How will I get around? Where will I eat?

In an instant, I caught myself: None of those things mattered. I would do anything to keep Kenny with us for as long as we could. We always supported each other and this was my time to prove it to him.

We went to the airport, had a bite to eat before our flight, and finally returned home about 10:00 p.m. What a roller coaster day!

Kenny's medical issues put us into a severe financial bind. I had to fight for every dollar from the insurance company. Extra co-payments to many doctors and bills for countless medications mounted. Limited monies came in, but payments for the mortgage and household bills still had to go out. Auntie and Uncle offered to cover our air fare and I accepted. I needed money for hotel fees, food, and other necessities while I was there. The gears of my brain turned and churned: What if he doesn't make it through the surgery? I would be away from home and my support system. I caught myself edging toward panic and immediately refocused. *One day at a time,* I told myself. *One day at a time.*

Easier said than done!

I contacted Kenny's work and told them about the surgery. They understood and wished us the best. Now I had to find a hotel to stay in. Our friends and family had done loads of research for me since I had so much on my plate. Dickie and Linda called and said that their family friend who was a Catholic priest, another Father Joe like our CYO friend, had relocated from Bedford, Mass., to Baltimore, Maryland. We had socialized with him on several occasions like christenings and weddings. They notified him about what was going on and he called us.

He proved to be a great resource for us. He was familiar with the hospital and made contacts for us. Saint Agnes Hospital dealt with a lot of cancer patients. They did have a Hope House where family members could stay while their loved ones were in the hospital, but they could only guarantee one week at a time. That wasn't going to work. The hospital staff said if he had to be in intensive care, I could stay in the family visitation room on the couch for a few days.

I figured my safest bet was to stay in a hotel while he was in the hospital. Then I would decide what to do when he got out. Knowing from experience how sick he always got after surgery, I could not imagine trying to care for him in a hotel room without a kitchen. Father Joe recommended that we see what happened and perhaps we could stay with him in his condo. That was so kind and so generous. I already felt better about going; we'd have a familiar face in our court.

Everyone supported this trip, but they were puzzled as to why we had to go out of state for the surgery. Why couldn't Kenny get the same surgery in Boston? they asked. If we wanted to research local surgeons, we had only about a month left before going to Baltimore.

There was a doctor at Mass General who did HIPEC. Why hadn't Dana Farber told us about him and this option? I called his office and made an appointment to see him the next week. His conversation was clinical and he did not express confidence in the HIPEC procedure.

I was wise enough to bring copies of all of Kenny's test results. When we presented Kenny's case to him, he said he had done only one of these surgeries, and that his patient, still in ICU, was not doing too well.

We told him about Dr. Esquivel and he laughed. He had trained under Dr. Esquivel. If Kenny were a member of his family, he said, he'd go to Baltimore, too, and have Esquivel do the operation. He reiterated that Esquivel was the best and the master of HIPEC.

Later we found out that HIPEC was too experimental and most hospitals didn't approve of it.

With that, we stuck with Dr. Esquivel. Off to Baltimore we went. I got two hotel rooms for a week. We were so blessed that Monica, Eric, Auntie, and Uncle insisted on coming with us.

On the day of the surgery, Father Joe picked us up and drove us to the hospital. We lit candles in the hospital chapel together. We all went in with Kenny before his operation and in came Dr. Esquivel. He explained to us that with Kenny's issues, morphine could not be used for pain management because it tends to shut down the bowel. He would use Fentanyl instead, which is much more effective for pain after bowel surgery. We were so grateful to him. Father Joe asked him to pray with us for Kenny. He responded with a big smile and said, "Of course I will. My first name is Jesus."

Uncle Bob & Auntie Lorraine

We all felt scared yet positive. Everyone said their goodbyes and made their way out of the small holding room, allowing Kenny and me a minute together, alone. We hugged each other. I reassured him that this was his best shot at living and staying with us longer. We smiled at each other and told each other how much we loved each other.

I held up for him and left him with a smile, but as soon as I got outside of the room, I fell apart. He might come through the operation okay, but we all needed a miracle. I embraced my family and was so thankful that they were with me. We put on our bravest faces to keep each other strong. Without saying a word, we all thought the same thing. This was a huge step with a high-risk factor.

The five of us sat in the waiting area, browsing through magazines, making small talk, snacking. I told everyone not to ask me to go to the cafeteria or for a walk. I wanted to stay right there for every update from the contact nurse. In half an hour, about 9:00 a.m., she reported that they had just begun the surgery.

By 2:00 p.m. the operation was due to be over. But about an hour later, around 10 a.m., the nurse came out and directed us into the family waiting room. Dr. Esquivel would join us in a moment.

Oh, my God! This was not good! What was going on? Although Kenny had been sick for so long, lately he had been feeling better and seemed strong enough to withstand this surgery. I trembled and felt faint that he hadn't survived.

In came the doctor with a serious face. He reported that when he opened Kenny up, he found far more cancer cells than the CT scan had indicated. At this point, the heated chemo would not be effective. He did think that if Kenny had a different specialized chemo for this specific cancer for the next six months, he could reassess him. If things improved, he could try the surgery again at a later date.

He apologized for the not-so-good news, but insisted that there was still hope. He knew a top GI oncologist at Massachusetts General Hospital in Boston. He recommended that this doctor become Kenny's new oncologist. He said we would talk tomorrow and he would set up an appointment with the MGH oncologist in a few weeks.

The doctor left me with a sympathetic hug. All of us cried in disbelief. We had all been so convinced Kenny had a good chance; we sure never expected this horrible news.

It was November 8, 2010, and the next day was Monica's 30th birthday. The kids were scheduled to fly back home the next day. They had families and jobs to attend to. Now what would happen? Our emotions were like a roller coaster—always up and down. I dreaded when Kenny had to find out about this turn of events. We were all a mess.

We visited him in recovery about an hour later. Although he was still groggy, he smiled and asked, "How did things go?" With fake, optimistic smiles, we pretended to be okay. We told him that the surgery couldn't be completed this time, but after more chemo, we could come back. Then he fell back asleep.

We were sure he was doomed. Where was Kenny's second chance?

We spent time with him when he was assigned to a room, but he was moaning in pain. This was the third time the doctors had gone into the same incision. We all went outside his room to plan. Kenny would be in the hospital for only a few days, after which he should be able to fly home. Auntie, Uncle, and Eric would go home now as scheduled. Monica would stay two extra days with me for moral support. She did not want to leave in case something happened to her dad on her birthday. I felt bad to keep her away from her family, but was so relieved to have her with me.

They all went back to the hotel and I slept on a recliner in Kenny's room. It was a rough night, but the next day he was more awake and felt a little better.

Dr. Esquivel came in the next day and explained everything again to Monica, Kenny, and me. Kenny never complained and did what he had to do. With fearful tears in his eyes, he agreed to go to Mass General. Every day he got a little stronger. Monica went home and Kenny and I prepared to do the same the next week.

How was he going to fly home? How would I manage both him and our luggage alone? I was so overwhelmed. Kenny's best friend, Lee, offered to fly down to Baltimore and help me get him home. We were so lucky to have such a wonderful support system. I had been there alone for a few days, so it was so great to see Lee's friendly face and receive his big hugs. He was shocked to see Kenny in this condition and how weak he was. They were best buds and were like brothers. Despite Kenny's troubles, it was great to see them together again, laughing and joking as they had always done.

Off we went to the Baltimore/Washington International Airport. Kenny still needed a wheelchair and walker. We called ahead for the handicapped section and the flight went well. Kenny went back and forth to the bathroom, but overall didn't do too badly. We flew into Manchester Airport and Eric was there to pick us up, along with most of the rest of the family—Karen, Drew, Jack, Molly, Monica, Jay, Emma, and Cameron. We were so surprised and thrilled to see them all. After what he had been through, Kenny needed to be in the loving arms of his family. It was such a relief to be back at 6 Sheila Avenue. Auntie and Uncle had prepared a nice dinner for us, one of Kenny's favorites: potatoes with sausages and meatballs in marinara sauce. We didn't bother to unpack and went to bed—totally exhausted.

Our house was filled with people in and out spending time with Kenny so I could go to work or the food shop. In particular, his cousin Paul, recently retired, came almost every day. They had grown up together and were only a year apart. Both loved cars. Paul had a 1968 Corvette. The two of them puttered in the garage, talked, and watched TV. I knew I didn't have to worry when they were together.

Kenny's sisters, Paula and Marsha, talked to us about having a fundraiser. At first, we were opposed to the idea, but it was quickly becoming obvious that keeping Kenny at home, with his bathroom issues, was a big problem. To accommodate him, we needed to install a half-bath in our bedroom. Reluctantly we agreed to the fundraiser. We thought now was a good time, while he was recovering, before he started his new chemo treatment plan.

The fundraiser was at the Chelmsford Elks. Marsha managed to get the hall donated. A parent at the preschool volunteered to be the DJ. Everyone organized raffles and food.

On the drive there, Kenny said, "Can you believe we are going to a cancer fundraiser and it is for me?" We were both in disbelief. We were so touched by the outpouring of people. There were about two hundred and fifty guests. It was wonderful to see all of our favorite people gathered together to support him, but we sure wished it was for a different cause. I have a beautiful album of family and friend photos to commemorate the evening. Several times later we looked through the pictures with fond memories.

Everyone's generosity enabled us to afford the half-bath construction and although prices for the project were much more than we had anticipated, it proved to be a godsend. We converted our closet into the half-bath and reconstructed the closet on the other side of the room.

Uncle had battled several bouts of pneumonia, which left nodules on his lungs. He still had chronic back pain and rheumatoid arthritis. When they lived here with us, I saw him daily, knew his symptoms, and was vigilant about his care. In Florida with their elderly friends, that was not always the case.

Most of their Floridian friends lived in Canada and went home in April, but Auntie and Uncle liked to stay until the end of May. Towards the end of April, Auntie said that Uncle Bob was not feeling well. Walking made him short of breath. I encouraged them to come home earlier, for the growing humidity wouldn't help Uncle's lungs. But they chose to stay. I hoped they would change their mind.

In the first week in May, Auntie called me, in near hysteria. She had just taken Uncle to the emergency room of their local hospital. They admitted him with possible pneumonia. He stayed there for a couple of days, but got worse. Because of a lack of communication between Auntie and doctors, he ended up in the intensive care unit. When she reported this, I asked Eric and Monica to fly down for the weekend and get the real picture of what was going on. I couldn't go yet. Kenny had just come off a round of chemo and felt lousy.

The kids flew down Friday night. They called me to report that Uncle was in bad shape. He was on a ventilator even though he had a "Do Not Resuscitate" order. The kids said, "Mom, if you want to see Uncle alive, you should come down." Kenny could not be left alone, so on Saturday morning, he and I flew together to Florida.

We went straight to the hospital immediately upon landing at Tampa International Airport. The kids had not exaggerated: things were awful. By then, Uncle's organs had shut down and he was in renal failure. It being the weekend, we couldn't reach any doctors. The end was near. My uncle had once owned a racehorse, and he loved to go to the track. Here, as he lay in the hospital, it seemed appropriate that the Kentucky Derby played faintly on the television in the background. Eric and I went to a funeral home and arranged for cremation (which was Uncle's wish). Auntie was still in denial.

On Monday, May 7, 2012, on a sunny spring day in a room with a view of the water, we finally reached Uncle's primary care doctor in Boston, who advised us to let him go peacefully. While we surrounded Uncle's bed, the attending physician pulled the plug. He passed quickly.

Poor Uncle Bob! None of us said it out loud, but we had all believed that Kenny was next. How much could this family endure?

The kids flew home. Kenny and I stayed with Auntie to wait for Uncle's ashes. It was a rough week and Auntie was distraught. The urn was delivered on Friday and we all flew home on Saturday. It was hard to help Auntie with her grief while we ourselves suffered as much.

On his better days, Kenny tinkered on his 1955 Chevy in his back garage. He kept all his pamphlets on house repairs, car contact info, and the titles to all of our vehicles in a big file cabinet. One day he came upstairs with a pink folder full of letters in his hands. When we had done our house addition, I had asked him to store our love letters downstairs, the ones he had sent me when we were teens. How fortunate that he found them now in one of his file cabinets! I glanced through them, smiling, grateful that they were once again in my possession. To this day, I find them a great comfort.

Kenny knew he could no longer go snowmobiling and decided to sell the snowmobiles and their trailer. Whatever money he got we could use for granite countertops in the kitchen. They sold quickly since they were in mint condition. The next month came the beautiful brown and beige granite countertops. We even bought new brown hardware for the cabinets, which Kenny installed. I loved them and hated them simultaneously: no more snowmobiling was not a good sign. But here we were again, working on our new normal.

We got the call for our scheduled appointment with Dr. Ryan and his team at Massachusetts General Hospital. We were curious to hear what he had to say. Paul came along as a third set of ears.

Upon entering the GI Cancer wing, we were greeted by two smiling receptionists, kind nurses calling their patients by their first and last names, and pleasant people in the waiting area. We discussed how no one is exempt from this horrible disease (no age, no race, no sex). After about ten minutes, we were called in to meet Dr. Ryan and his nurse practitioner. In came the tall, handsome doctor, about fifty years old, with his pretty, female assistant.

After a brief exam, Dr. Ryan asked us to summarize the past two years. Even though he had reviewed all the test results, this case was complicated. He was blunt that the cancer is smarter than chemo and eventually cancer usually wins. Dr. Esquivel's expertise was to be commended, but he told us up front he was convinced that HIPEC was not the way to go.

He agreed to take Kenny on as a patient. More cell mutations had to be analyzed. He described the creation of an individualized chemo cocktail. He and his team were cautiously optimistic and reassured us that he would do all he could to give Kenny more time, while trying to provide some quality of life during the process. With Kenny's approval, he ordered his own set of tests and bloodwork.

He was brutally honest that this was a tough regimen. Kenny would be infused every three weeks, giving him more time in between to recuperate from the side effects.

Kenny's long-term disability was about to run out. Dr. Ryan agreed to sign the paperwork for Social Security Disability. We were off and running with a new plan. The Yawkey Cancer Center became our new hope.

Hope is a funny thing. Every few months what we hoped for shifted and we'd have to head down a different road. We'd hope the medical professionals had made a mistake, hope the pain would ease up, hope the chemo treatments would work better, hope their side effects would subside, hope he could still eat, hope he could maintain his weight. On and on we hoped.

At Brooksby Village, the human resources department, Kenny's bosses, and his co-workers were beyond amazing: They visited often and sent care packages, floral arrangements, and meals. We were so lucky that he had been surrounded by wonderful nurses, doctors and thoughtful co-workers who really cared during his illness.

He filed for Social Security Disability and he was approved. But with Kenny no longer on the payroll at Brooksby, we were not covered by medical insurance. I got a call from Brooksby's director, who said they had had a team meeting about Kenny's situation, and that one of the assistant directors was coming over to our house to talk with us about a plan they wanted to implement. We had no idea what this meant.

The next day the Brooksby representative came with well-wishes for us and a warm embrace for Kenny. It had been a while since he had seen Kenny. He couldn't hide his shock to see how fragile Kenny was. At that point Kenny had to use a walker to get around. His decline had been gradual for me, but it surprised most people.

The Brooksby family had come together with a course of action. The only way for Erickson Communities Corporate Office to keep Kenny's medical coverage active for a while was if his co-workers were willing to donate their sick days and vacation time. Our eyes were filled with tears of gratitude that these marvelous people were willing to do this for him. The assistant director himself said he had accrued several months of time he would probably never use, so he would donate one month. We were so touched by this generosity. Keeping our medical coverage would be one huge worry off our shoulders, even if only for a while.

Brooksby stayed in touch with me and sent me a monthly report of how many hours were allotted. In the beginning, we were good for at least six months. It turned into nine. He would get paid and we both would keep our medical insurance. We needed to stay with Blue Cross Blue Shield, since all of Kenny's doctors were all in the BCBS network through Mass General Hospital.

We could not get over how generous these people were. They lifted a huge burden off our shoulders. We were so thankful! The money situation was under control as he began his new chemo the next week. This kept us solvent for almost a year.

Sometimes I'd sit alone in our TV room and gaze at our old family pictures on the wall, then glance over at him. I could not believe what my tall, handsome, robust husband had been reduced to. I would quickly re-direct my thoughts to see him still as the man I loved, the father of my children. I always took my marriage vows seriously, but now more than ever, I thought about the *"in sickness and in health"* vow. I never expected to be so severely tested by this phrase.

When the insurance ended, we were on our own. I was naïve to Social Security Disability. Initially I assumed that once Kenny was accepted, he would have state medical coverage. Much to our shock, that was not the case. (At the same time, I learned that I had to get my own individual medical insurance since I was self-employed. Social Security covered only the individual.) A patient had to have been on Social Security Disability for two years before he or she qualified for free medical benefits.

I was disgusted with a system that turned its back on a man who worked all his life, paid his bills, and provided for his family. It forced us into the COBRA plan, which was way too expensive. The salt in the wound was the stories we've all heard, about irresponsible people who always make the wrong choices and were not productive members of society, yet who are always eligible for state and federal hand-outs. It was not fair. But life was not always fair.

It was Friday, his assigned chemo day, and off we went to Boston, wracked by every emotion possible. People had sent us dozens of prayer cards, crosses, and angels. I learned quickly that Saint Peregrine was the Cancer Saint. It was my idea to read one of the prayer cards every time prior to Kenny's chemo. He reluctantly did it at first but it soon became our ritual. We had nothing to lose, only to gain.

Kenny's experience at other hospitals was with regimented workers who had no people skills. It was refreshing to find that those at this facility were welcoming. They greeted us with a kind smile. Although I know that might not make a difference, medically, to the patient, after all Kenny had been through, it made a lot of difference in our hearts and minds. The humane reception from this team was encouraging. He was no longer just a number, but a living human being fighting for his life. Now he had a team working toward the same goal. The chemo was brutal, but knowing it was killing malignant cancer cells gave us both a boost of confidence.

We often saw the same people every time we were in the infusion room. We caregivers—spouses, family members, close friends—often met in the cafeteria over lunch or a cup of tea, making the time go by quicker. Misery does love company, and our mutual conversations were often sad, but this community of medical staff and patients made Kenny and me feel less alone. So many others were going through the same challenges, and the sharing helped to restore our spirits.

One day I thought I recognized a woman having treatment. I approached her and discovered that it was Jean, with whom I worked at one of my first part-time college jobs, a dress shop. She had pancreatic cancer and had the same doctor as Kenny. He recognized her husband since they worked together at Polaroid. It was a small world.

This was more than a coincidence and we all chatted together even socialized a little when we could and comforted each other. We laughed and cried together and we all agreed we had been living the American dream as husbands, wives, fathers, mothers, grandmothers and grandfathers, but cancer ruined it all. We never thought it could happen to us, but it did.

Kenny couldn't drive anymore, so he turned over the title of his 55 Chevy to Eric. He wanted his son and grandsons to continue his legacy by driving his car and exhibiting it at car shows. He gave Monica his Chevy Tahoe SUV. This bigger car accommodated her needs to transport her children, and they'd be safer in it.

Kenny had his regular chemo treatment and waited for those three weeks in between for scan results. Once again, our lives were on hold. Before, we had socialized to some degree, but now his immune system was so shot, we rarely did. Our friends and family always came by for short visits, but he usually had to excuse himself, to go to bed for a nap.

This MGH experience was grueling. Sometimes both sides of his port were blocked. Sometimes his blood counts were so low, he needed a blood transfusion. Now what used to take six or seven hours took ten or eleven hours. One time security had to wheel him out because the cancer center had closed for the night. But every scan showed improvement!

Dr. Esquivel and Dr. Ryan conferred about Kenny's case. They agreed that his condition warranted another try with the HIPEC process. Off we went again to Baltimore in July of 2013.

The headquarters of Erickson Communities, the corporation that owned Brooksby Village, was in Baltimore. When Kenny's Brooksby family, which was so emotionally involved with us, found out about his chance for another surgery, they arranged for us to use an apartment on their Maryland campus for the duration of our stay. This included all meals and shuttle service from the airport, and back and forth to Saint Agnes Hospital for me and our family and friends. This was a huge relief. Neither of us would have to worry about how we would live for six weeks. Their generosity and compassion stunned us. "Thank you" was not enough.

Before we left, Brooksby held a little luncheon for us so Kenny could visit with all his co-workers. He was happy to see them in person, and to thank them for their charity. It was bittersweet for him be just a visitor at a facility in which he had been such an integral part, such an asset.

For this Baltimore trip, Monica and Kenny's sister, Paula, came with us, to be with me during the surgery. Auntie stayed in Woburn to take care of our cats, Sasha and Sheba. Eric stayed home to work, but planned to fly down a few days after the operation. Kenny's cousin Linda offered to come down to spend a few days with me, too. For the trip home Paul would come down to help us get home. How lucky were we!

It was July and other than part-time summer camp, the preschool was closed for the season. We had already held graduation and had enrolled students for the Fall. My staff did a great job taking care of the day-to-day business at WOW, now that Monica was so occupied with us.

We were all packed and ready for this next adventure. We were still in disbelief that Kenny had another shot at this. He and I had to be there a day early to settle into the apartment and do his pre-op. Monica and Paula would fly down the next day.

The night before we left, Kenny and I had another heart-to-heart. This surgery had the potential to be our last time together. Saying goodbyes for us was always painful. Kenny knew how proud I was of him and how brave I thought he was. I cried in his arms, saying, "I thought we were going to grow old together." Kenny, in his always common-sense wisdom, said, "We have, maybe just not for as long as we thought it would be." He apologized to me for ruining the good life we had, which I chided him for suggesting, and expressed his gratitude for having me in his life and loving him as I did. We both hugged and cried. I asked him if he was afraid and he said, "Not yet," which I thought was an insightful statement. We regrouped and went to bed, ready to meet the next challenge down the road.

As promised, the Brooksby van was waiting for us at the airport and brought us to the Baltimore campus of Erickson Communities. We were greeted like VIPs by the director and some of his staff. They welcomed us with open arms. We got the tour, saw the dining hall, met workers, and saw indoor and outdoor spaces for relaxing and all the extra activity rooms for the residents. We were given a code number and badges to exempt us from any fees, even the gift shop. He brought us to our studio apartment, which was adorable. It had a queen-sized bed and a pull-out couch with a full kitchen. A welcome package on the kitchen table was filled with fruits and snacks. There was a little variety store where we could shop, using our code. They also gave us a wheelchair, walker, and cane from their Rehabilitation Department. This was one of the nicest things anyone had ever done for us. It was such a relief to have a roof over our heads and a home base.

We unpacked and got settled. I also brought a hospital bag with essentials for both of us. We called for the van and went to his appointment at the hospital. The doctor's nurse showed us a huge bulletin board with all kinds of cards thanking the doctor and his staff for their hospitality, pictures of success stories and their families, and lots of inspirational quotes. Everything was so encouraging! The focal point of this wall was a map of the United States with several push pins in all of the states. She explained that each push pin represented a patient who successfully had HIPEC. Now our goal was to have a pushpin in the state of Massachusetts to represent Kenny. It was cool and motivational.

They conducted lots of other pre-op testing, then he was a go. Monica and Paula arrived the next day. The van took them to our Erickson apartment, which became our new home away from home. Kenny couldn't eat pre-surgery, but he encouraged the three of us to go to the dining hall for supper. We all had a nice meal, talked, and tried to be positive for each other. The four of us spent a nice night together, watching TV and relaxing as much as we could.

The next morning, we were on our way back to Saint Agnes Hospital for the big day. I gripped my small statue of Saint Agnes in my fist. This time we were familiar with the hospital, the process, and the pre-op waiting rooms. Dr. Esquivel came in and said, "Let's do this!" and off he went.

The three of us deliberately sat in different chairs from when we were there before. I wanted everything to be dissimilar to last time, especially the result. The informing nurse came out to report that the operation had begun. About an hour later she came out again: it was a green light to begin the heated chemotherapy. Thank God! Two hours later it was still underway. The hot chemo sat in the abdomen for the next hour, and they closed him up in the final hour.

The doctor came out finally and reported that Kenny was okay, his vitals were fine, and the operation had gone well. That new six-month chemo cocktail regimen definitely had killed more cancer cells, giving the surgeon the confidence to proceed with the HIPEC. He reiterated that recovery would be rough, but didn't believe Kenny needed to be in ICU. He'd have a private room, so I could stay and sleep with him. His nurse was assigned to only two patients.

Kenny had been given an epidural along with the Fentanyl pump to control the pain. We waited a few hours for them to bring him up to his room. He was still asleep when we went to see him, so I encouraged the girls to go back to the apartment to eat and sleep. They reluctantly did, but I assured them that I was here with him to take care of him. Little did I know what a tall order that turned out to be.

About an hour later Kenny woke up from the anesthesia. He could barely open his eyes. I told him the surgery was a success, I was here with him, and I loved him. The nurse was in and out, but taking vitals caused him to moan and scream from the pain. Even the stethoscope hurt. She assured me that all of this was normal, post-surgery, but it sure didn't sound normal to me.

The night was brutal for him and he was no better in the morning. He was heavily drugged from the meds, but when the doctor came and told him about the success of the operation, Kenny managed to give us a little smile. The girls came back to the hospital and were taken aback by the degree of his pain.

The medical staff promised that he would improve every day, but his progress was so slow we couldn't see it. We took shifts holding his hand but even our gentle touch hurt. The next day he was awake and talking a little, and they propped him up in a chair like a ragdoll, surrounded by soft pillows. By the time the girls went home, he was a little better. I put on a strong front for them, but inside, I was petrified to be alone there without them. Luckily in two days Linda was coming. By then they tried to get him up to walk, but he could not do it.

When Linda arrived, I saw the terror and disbelief in her face when she saw how sick he still was. Actually, when she came, on that fourth day post-surgery, he was getting worse. The doctor was a little surprised that he was still registering his pain level at ten and that he was too weak to walk. His concern troubled me. The next two days were horrible and now I was afraid that although he made it through the surgery, he might not make it through recovery.

It was such a comfort to have a family member to vent to. Linda was great and I was thrilled to have her with me. She admitted to me later she had feared that he would die while she was there with me.

By the time Linda was scheduled to go home Kenny had improved. He could sit up, eat a little, and walk the hallways with assistance. Eric was coming down for the weekend and I was grateful that he didn't have to witness his dad as sick as he had been. Eric had already seen some of his father's worst days.

In came Eric and Kenny greeted him with a big smile. By then he was capable of receiving a hug. The highlight of Eric's trip to Baltimore was walking Kenny down the hallway to the bulletin board so Kenny could place a blue pushpin into the state of Massachusetts. We all clapped. To this day I've never looked at a pushpin the same way. No one but us knew what it took to place that pushpin into that bulletin board.

Nurse Robin & Kenny at Saint Agnes Hospital

After two weeks Kenny was released from the hospital and we spent a few peaceful weeks in the apartment while he recuperated. By the second week I could wheel him around the campus. Sometimes we ate in the dining hall. Sometimes we sat in the recreation hall for private time together without doctors, nurses, and hospital rooms. We were happy to sit on the couch together, sleep in a bed together, and anticipate a return to married life.

Paul flew down to help us get home. He spent a few days with us and then we got the green light to leave. Again, it was great to see them hang out together. We landed at Logan where Eric met us. Everyone was at the house to welcome him home.

It was so good to be home with a good outcome. This was chemo break-time for him and he needed it. He could barely eat any solid foods yet, but little by little he progressed.

Upon our return home, MGH agreed to handle his incision care and take his staples out. Dr. Esquivel was instrumental in making this happen. He had many medical contacts who held him in high esteem and respected him. We were so lucky to have him helping us.

Surprisingly Kenny gained some weight and strength. I went back to work, we ran errands and shopped for food together again, and did small projects around the house. For about a year, things were so much better. He resumed the chemo treatments, every three weeks, throughout the winter and spring months, but it was not too bad. We were cautiously optimistic, but afraid to be too positive. We were finally getting our lives back.

Kenny and I continued to attend the cancer support group through the years, where we had made new friends. The group helped both of us to learn with other people how to face the same kinds of challenges. The head of the group gave everyone lots of informational materials and always had encouraging words. The monitor taught us to look at cancer as a chronic illness and not a death sentence. She gave out buttons that said, "Cancer sucks!" No truer words have ever been spoken. She would say it was okay to have a pity party, but do not have a cup of tea with it. So true!

We had encouraged Auntie to go back to Florida for the winter months. We didn't believe that she should deprive herself of her winter in Florida because of us. We talked over the phone with her a few times a week. I never told Auntie the full truth about how Kenny was doing. It would have crushed her. He could eat and drink little, but vomited frequently and often had raging diarrhea and fatigue. But he always did his best to reassure her that he was okay.

As if things could not get worse, one day when Kenny was in the shower, he called to me loudly, distressed. The surgeons had gone through the same incision four times, and they had warned us that the tissue around the scar was very delicate. Now the skin separated and his insides were exposed. We rushed back to MGH. They cleaned out the wound and packed it with gauze, and provided us with a wound-care nurse who came to the house every other day to pack him, to avoid infection. It had to heal from the inside out. Medical supplies were delivered to the house weekly. He had to wrap himself in a Saran-like plastic sheeting in order to take a shower. The nurse assured us that although the gap was about four inches deep, the body has an amazing ability to heal itself.

After four months the insurance no longer paid for the visiting nurse, so she taught me how to do it. I sucked it up and did what I had to. If anyone had ever told me that I'd have to do this, I would have said, "No way!" I grew to hate the phrase that God never gives you more than you can handle, even if it was true. It took two more horrendous months for the incision to heal over and close.

Cancer once again reared its ugly head, about nine months later. Kenny was so discouraged. We went back to MGH in fear and anxiety. They did a scan and confirmed that the cancer was back. The oncologist ordered a colonoscopy; it had spread to the large bowel. He had predicted some time before that the cancer would outsmart the chemo, and that was exactly what was happening.

Kenny had a tube put into his stomach to drain the bile buildup, and he had a PICC-line put in for additional fluids. The only option now was an experimental clinical trial. I thought Kenny would say he was done, but to my surprise he didn't. He wanted to try it.

One night when neither of us could sleep I got out the pink folder from our closet and we reviewed our love notes. We took a trip down memory lane and we laughed and cried together. We found old cards and letters he had given to me. I realized the innocence of our love and how it blossomed. There was a poem he had written about me for an English assignment. Kenny—a poet? No way! But he was proud of it and I was deeply touched.

Kenny had bought a 1932 Hudson hot rod as a retirement project. For a while he had still been able to putt around there in his garage, but lately not so much. A huge turning point for him was when he tore down slips of paper from his informational bulletin board and said it was time to sell the car. Walking by that hot rod, after his diagnosis, had haunted me for years, but the thought of not seeing it was even more frightening.

We came upstairs to our kitchen table where we always celebrated good things or mourned bad things with a cup of tea. He talked about selling our commercial building on 905 Main that housed the preschool. He didn't want to leave me with that huge responsibility. I hesitantly agreed because it was true, one less thing for me to deal with. We decided to put it on the market soon. Reality was really sinking in. We passed papers on the property on March 6, 2014, to a local Woburn businessman. It was a sad day for both of us. This was supposed to be our retirement income, not this bad dream.

During this period of the clinical trial, Kenny lost his hair. Now we had the visual reminder, on the outside, of what was happening to him on the inside. He was never a hat person, but I bought him knit hats and scully caps, which he reluctantly wore. But they made him feel more comfortable, and with visitors, the kids, and the grandkids, it was less disturbing.

Things were going downhill quickly and nothing was working for him. He had lost more weight and was much weaker. His body was no longer able to process nutrients. One Sunday morning he almost collapsed while shoveling snow in February 2014. Again we rushed him to the hospital. It was the beginning of the end.

March 31st was his 61st birthday. All the kids and grandkids came and slept over. We got Chinese food and he put egg foo yung, one of his favorites, in the nutribullet® blender to puree it so he could digest it. We all celebrated what we all knew was his last birthday. Some of them lounged in our indoor hot tub and that was the last night we ever used it. It was a great night of memories. In the morning, he insisted on cooking bacon, eggs, and pancakes for all of us. It exhausted him, and when everyone left, he spent the rest of the day in bed.

One night he talked to me about wanting to stay home. This was where he wanted to take his last breath. I wanted him to have his wish, but couldn't imagine myself living in the house if he passed away there. He also stressed that he wanted me to move on and not be alone, to find someone new to love. I didn't want to hear any of this. It was too much to absorb, too soon.

Everyday his health declined. We were constantly in training to administer the tasks that kept Kenny alive. Visiting nurses of various specialties checked in every other day. A small refrigerator in our computer room held the seven bags of nutrients—his liquid diet—delivered to the house weekly. We hooked up Kenny to an IV bag at night and disconnected it in the morning. Blood tests were weekly to determine the custom mixture Kenny needed. I made protein shakes for him and sprinkled protein powder over everything, in an effort to help him sustain his weight.

I took to eating my meals in the TV room because I felt guilty eating solid food in front of Kenny. Knowing that he couldn't enjoy a real meal anymore made my food tasteless, too.

Every week a new problem cropped up. After six weeks, and repeated advice to return to the hospital for more tests, Kenny finally gave in, and back we went to MGH. We were conflicted: We wanted to get to the bottom of this, but at the same time, we didn't want to know.

The tests at the hospital gave us bad news and worse news. The nutrient bags no longer worked. People from the Palliative Care Division came to Kenny's room to discuss our options, but we were just about out of those. A few days later, we headed for home, having arranged for Hospice Care at the house. No one said a word, but it was obvious that this was his last trip to Massachusetts General Hospital.

Eric and Monica rotated staying with me at night so we could keep Kenny home. Although he didn't want a hospital bed, we were forced to get one. We abutted it up against our bed. Day by day he got worse. We pushed the button on his Fentanyl pump every fifteen minutes to keep the pain level manageable. Our hospice nurse said that he might have to go to a hospice house because a cancer this bad was almost impossible to manage in a home setting. I tried not to believe that, but day after day I realized that she was right. We could not keep up with the pain and now he could barely make it into the bathroom.

It was coming up on our 40th wedding anniversary and the kids thought he was hanging on for that. April 26th was a horrific day so Eric went out and bought two anniversary cards—one for his dad and one for me. We lied to Kenny and told him this was our Anniversary Day. It was really the 28th, but Kenny was too sick to take any notice of the calendar anymore. I gave him my card and when he saw the other card, he called out for a pen. Eric gave him a pen, and as wobbly as he was, he signed the envelope, not the card. "Forty forever, do not forget my poem, Love Ken." I put it in a frame. It is my most precious possession. The kids' theory of Kenny passing on our anniversary proved to be wrong. The 28th came and went and still he hung on.

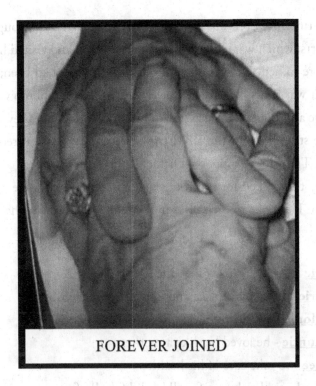

FOREVER JOINED

Lee always came by after work and so did Eric. One day they were both at the house when Kenny had to go to the bathroom. We helped him onto the toilet, and after about two minutes he blanked out and became limp. The three of us panicked and thought he had died. We shook him and after about a minute he came to as if nothing had ever happened. We were all petrified. Kenny had no recollection of this. It was so bizarre. We figured his blood pressure must have dropped.

On Friday, the nurse informed me that it was only a matter of a few days for Kenny. She asked to talk to him about transferring to the Kaplan Care Dimensions House in Danvers, where they could control his pain with IV pain management. The Fentanyl was no longer effective. To my surprise, Kenny agreed.

Everyone in our families and friend circles would want to say their goodbyes. The kids set right to it, to notify them all, and scheduled each to come on Saturday, the next day. It was open-house style, with staggered times for everyone to have a brief visit. Everyone brought meals and desserts, which was a blessing for the rest of us, and visited him while he lay there in bed. He was much more alert than he had been; I'm sure he knew it was time. He smiled as everyone posed for a photo with him.

Dickie and Linda had been vacationing in Florida, but they flew back and came straight from the airport to see Kenny. We captured one last picture of The Three Amigos—Dickie, Paul and Kenny.

Kenny then asked for specific people to come alone so he could talk with them. He spoke to each of us individually. This is what he told each of us:

> **Me** - I was the love of his life
> **Eric** - to take his place and look after the family
> **Monica** - to try to be happy and healthy
> **Auntie** - he loved her like a mother
> **Lee** - to take care of his health
> **Paul** - to thank him for all he did for all of us

He didn't go to Danvers until Monday, when a bed became available. Monica rode in the ambulance with us and Eric followed in the car. It was a haunting thought to realize when I returned to 6 Sheila Avenue, he would be gone and I would be alone. As the paramedics put him in the ambulance, he whispered, "Car." We knew exactly what he meant. Eric opened up the garage door so Kenny could behold his beloved 55 Chevy one last time. It made us all heart-sick.

When we arrived at the hospice house, I glanced outside the ambulance to see what it looked like. Kenny was out of it, but it would have pleased him to see what a nice bright day it was, with blooming flowers, birds chirping, and bunches of cattails. He loved to be out in nature.

They brought us to a back room with a view. All I saw as we walked through the hallways were the rooms on either side, occupied by tearful people waiting for their loved ones to pass. It was like a big funeral home.

The décor was lovely, but the atmosphere was morbid. "How did Kenny and I end up here?" I thought. But here we were.

There was a twin bed in Kenny's room that I could use. I had brought a few of his favorite things—model cars, rosary beads, and family photos—in an effort to make this death room a little more homey. We had dressed him in his favorite flannel pajamas to keep him warm. A staff member mentioned to me that no food was available for family members, so I would have to arrange my meals to be brought in from outside.

By now Kenny couldn't speak at all and was in a semi-coma. They rotated him every few hours to prevent bed sores. He took no food or drink, except for medications to control pain. No fever checks, blood pressure, or suction. I had no idea that death had so many phases; each day he passed through one of them. He was always a tough and determined guy, and his death reflected how he lived his life. Family and close friends came regularly to comfort me.

While we were at the Kaplan House, the family asked what they could do to make it easier for me when I finally returned home. I told them to please remove the hospital bed, the medical supplies, and the drugs from the house. I didn't want to see any reminder of Kenny's illness. Monica and Lorraine took care of that and I was grateful.

On Friday. Paul and Lee spent most of the day with me. Kenny's nurse kept insisting that it would be better for Kenny if I left the room. She said that he was holding onto life for my sake, and that if I wasn't there, he would allow himself to pass peacefully. But I did not want to leave him. I knew Kenny far better than she did. We had had a lifetime together; she had known him—in a comatose state—for four days. I needed to be with him at the end, and I knew he needed me to be with him at the end. No way I would let him die alone.

After dinner Paul's wife, Carol, and Lee's wife, Lorraine, came to be with us. People had brought me food but I hadn't eaten all day. I sat with a breakfast sandwich at a little round table near his bed, but I couldn't eat it. Paul sat in a chair and Lee pressed his pain pump. All of a sudden, Lee yelled out to me and Paul jumped out of his chair. Carol and Lorraine, who had been chatting outside of the room, ran in, and the nurse rushed in to attend to Kenny. But he was gone. Time of death: 8:47 p.m. on May 9, 2014.

The hospice house called for the undertaker. I asked him to wait for a couple hours so everyone could say their goodbyes. I immediately called Eric and Monica, and they came together. I called Auntie, and Carol went to pick her up. Paula and Marsha came, too.

We gathered around him for the last time. Each of us had a brief, private moment before going out of the room.

I was the last to exit. I climbed into his bed and held him until coldness filled his body and chilled me. In my heart, that was the only way I could accept that he was gone. Part of me felt relieved for him that his suffering was over, but another part of me couldn't grasp the concept that I would never see my beloved Kenny again, not on this earth. The puzzle pieces had slipped away, never to reunite until we meet again in the afterlife.

Leaving him was brutal. We all walked out into the parking lot, numb. I rode home with Lorraine. The ride back to Woburn was solemn and silent. The kids walked into the house with me, for the first time ever without their dad. All the horrific medical equipment was gone, sheets and towels thrown out, medicines disposed of discreetly. I never again wanted to think about those last days of pure hell for him.

Lorraine had spread a new comforter on the bed. It seemed to refresh the room.

During all this, Eric and Monica had been away from their families for weeks. I insisted that they go home and be with their kids and spouses. Lorraine stayed overnight with me and we talked all night. Finally talked out, I cried myself to sleep in the wee hours. In the morning, Lorraine made phone calls for me, prepared food, and ran errands for things I needed in the house.

By 10:00 a.m. on Saturday, the house was jammed with family and friends. People brought flowers and food. In and out they flowed until after dark, paying their condolences. It was tough to greet people, especially my five grandkids, my daughter-in-law and son-in-law, without Kenny at my side. Their hugs and reassuring words consoled me. I was exhausted but welcomed the company. When everyone left, I would be alone.

My dear friend Lorraine and me

Over the course of the last year of Kenny's life, it seemed that every time we glanced at a clock in the morning or night, it read 9:05. We thought this represented the address of WOW, 905 Main Street. I had been afraid that he would pass on September 5th, the fifth day of the ninth month. Instead, he passed on May 9, 2010, the ninth day of the fifth month. The numbers were reversed. Even now when I glance at the clock, I often see those same numbers. It can't be coincidence.

The next day, Sunday, was Jack and Drew's First Communion. I got dressed—it felt good in a way to dress so nicely—and Auntie and I went. That's what Kenny would have wanted. I put on my fake smile and pretended I was all right. Of course, I was not. It would take time, a lot of time. Family surrounded me all day, but as soon as I got back home, reality set in.

What was I going to do with myself? I was 60 years old and a widow, a title I had never wanted to hold. How could I be Linda without Kenny? People sent letters and encouraging poems, spiritual and sympathy cards to comfort me. Everyone was so kind, which helped briefly, but soon the sadness settled in for good.

The next week I did not sleep well. Weirdly, anticipating the delivery of his ashes kept me both sad and excited. One day I got the call announcing that he was coming home. The next morning the doorbell rang, and out in the driveway stood a big black town car. The nice gentleman at the door carried a box with the urn within, and a package of prayer cards and thank-you cards. He came in and placed the box on my kitchen table. After I escorted him out, I found a pair of scissors and opened up the box. Inside was the beautiful tan marble urn that I had picked out. I pulled it out reverently. It was tall and sleek, as he had been. I hugged it for a moment. The moment was not in the least bit freaky, but more a moment of relief, of closure.

Kenny was home again, with me.

Kenny's new home was a small corner table in the bedroom. Along with his urn, I had ordered a companion urn, a tiny replica of the big one. I could keep a bit of Kenny in my pocketbook, clutch him in my hand, or set him on the coffee table to keep me company wherever I sat. For the first year, every single night I slept with the companion urn, embracing my Kenny. That may seem bizarre to some, but to me that was a vital part of my grieving process. For the entirety of the four years of his sickness, I had rarely slept through the night. I had always worried about him; most nights he was up and down, in and out of the bathroom. Now, with the help of melatonin and my companion urn, I slept.

Seeing Kenny's obituary in the paper was surreal. It was hard to process. Prior to his service I had gone to the Paper Store because I wanted the kids and grandkids to have something special to remember him by. I bought Monica, Auntie, Karen, Emma, Molly, and Kenny's sisters each a musical jewelry box and gave Eric, Jay, Drew, Jack, Cameron, Lee, Paul and Roger each a blue, toy-model 55 Chevy. I also bought one of each for myself.

The day of Kenny's Mass was the first time that I had ever closed down World of Wonder. All of my WOW parents supported my decision. My entire staff and several present and past families attended, showing a deep measure of their regard.

That Tuesday morning, May 20, 2010, Eric and Monica came to pick up Auntie and me in Kenny's Chevy. His urn sat in my lap as we drove to Saint Robert's Church in Andover. We brought him into the church and the priest showed us where to place the urn during the Mass. Collages of family, friends and coworkers decorated the front of the church. It broke my heart, with both joy and heartache, to see our grandkids all dressed in blue, to honor their Papa, and so upset at their loss. Kenny had requested no wake, so the service was where mourners gathered.

As Eric, Monica, and I stood at the back of the church, mourners filed in and greeted us. Lines and lines of visitors wrapped around the church and down the sidewalk. Brooksby's vans shuttled people to the church for the service. It was truly beyond belief. He had influenced and helped so many people during his life and everyone had gathered to honor the wonderful man he was. The way he lived his life was the way he was now remembered.

We had encouraged everyone to wear Kenny's favorite color. The church was filled with a glorious cloud of blue, the music began, and we all tearfully walked into our front pews. The altar was full of blue hydrangeas, his favorite flower. Then all eyes were on Eric as he carried his father in his strong arms down the aisle and placed the urn on the podium. I had been to so many funerals in my life and mourned others. I never wanted to be the grieving wife sitting in the first row with whom everyone sympathized.

I had asked Lee and Paul to speak but they had to decline since they were so distraught. I respected that. Dickie and Linda delivered a wonderful eulogy. The kids and grandkids lit candles during the beautiful

Mass. There was not a dry eye in the church for the songs "Ava Maria" and "On Eagle's Wings." Sobs punctuated the service. I was numb through it.

We had booked the Tewksbury Country Club for his celebration of life. Kenny loved the wood-clad ballroom there. We knew the manager, so he agreed to let us park Kenny's 55 Chevy with the hood up in the entrance way, so as people passed by, they could admire it. This was his last car show. About one hundred people joined us. His favorite oldies music played softly in the background. Everything was personalized to him.

Linda suggested that his closest friends should bring an item that represented his life, make a comment, and put it in a "Backpack to Heaven." There was a list of about thirty packers and thirty items, such as car magazines, a wrench, lug nuts, a wedding band, a tea bag, a favorite CD, Oreo cookies, and Hostess cream-filled cupcakes. Each friend stood at the podium and spoke in their own words how their item represented Kenny's life to them. It was touching to hear everyone pay homage to him; it gave me the chills.

People enjoyed a buffet table, loaded with appetizers and entrees. There was a coffee station with cookies and pastries. Lots of special people chatted throughout the pleasant yet solemn atmosphere. It was so comforting. Everything went as we had hoped.

Lee insisted on carrying the urn out of the reception. He placed Kenny in the trunk of the Chevy, and Eric headed for the house with the five grandkids. They barely got a half mile up onto Route 38 when the car stalled and died. It had to be towed from Tewksbury to Woburn. We all laughed when we heard about it. Kenny had warned Eric about six months prior that the clutch needed adjustment. Truly, it was Kenny's way of letting us know he was still with us!

People close to us and some of the kids' friends came back to Sheila Avenue to hang out with me. With everyone leaving and with the realization that my life alone was now a reality, I felt totally out of control. Now it was Auntie, alone downstairs in her in-law apartment, and me, alone upstairs in my house.

Adding to my pressure, graduation rehearsals at World of Wonder were scheduled for the next day. Staff and parents had been so wonderful to me throughout Kenny's illness that I felt the right thing for me to do was to be there as the school's director. So, I pulled myself together and presented the graduates their diplomas on stage. I made it through the day, but it was exhausting to pretend to be okay but I really was not. I was proud of myself that I did so without falling apart.

After Kenny's passing, I needed time to regroup. What were my next steps? My life turned into a calling center, as I made and received endless phone calls to Social Security, life insurance companies, and medical centers. The copies of Kenny's death certificate really did me in, but without this document, nothing could be finalized.

My biggest dilemma was who would Linda be without Kenny? How would I continue to live my life? I felt survivor's guilt every time I laughed, smiled, or experienced the least bit of enjoyment. It was hard for me to figure out why I was still here and he was not. I had been in a relationship most of my life and did not know how to be happy or make my way on my own. Kenny had told me, not long before he died, that he did not want me to be alone; he said I had a lot to contribute to a relationship. I didn't want to accept it then, but he was giving me permission to find happiness with another, if I wanted.

I couldn't think about that now. I couldn't imagine sharing my life with anyone else. Kenny was my all-in-all and always would be. It wasn't easy to be the one left behind, to pick up the pieces. It was terrifying!

My first trip to Home Depot by myself was overwhelming. In one of the aisles, a rush of anxiety flooded me. I put back whatever it was I had intended to buy and ran out of the store. That was Kenny's realm, not mine. Simple tasks like walking past the men's department in a clothing store or pumping gas at the gas station stressed me out.

In addition, for so long, I had not had the leisure to shop or run errands without rushing, without worrying about getting back to Kenny. Now, I had nothing but time.

One beautiful summer morning with the sun glistening, I sat out on the deck with a cup of tea. The wind chimes tinkled in a gentle breeze. When I glanced into the pines that lined the backyard, something ruby-colored flew out of the trees toward me. A bright red cardinal flared its wings to slow its approach and perched on the deck railing. It sat for a few moments, looking at me without fear, before it flew off on its own business.

A popular folk legend or superstition is that the cardinal represents the spirit of a deceased loved one, and you are lucky if you see one, for that means that your loved one is watching over you, and you are not alone. The confidence of this bird, as it stayed to observe me as I observed it, convinced me that it was Kenny, come to visit and comfort me. Superstition or not, I was greatly comforted.

Another superstition is that when a penny appears randomly, it's a sign that our deceased loved one placed it there for us to find, so we'll know that they are okay. Enough pennies began to appear randomly that I collected them and keep them in a jar that Monica bought for me. These are my *Pennies from Heaven*; they remind me that my Kenny is close by.

While Kenny worked at Brooksby Village he did maintenance inside and outside. There was a beautiful courtyard for the residents. On nice days, the CNAs wheel out the residents to enjoy the nature of birds, trees and flowers, and to bask in the sun. Kenny wanted them to have more to see and revel in, so he proposed to his boss to make a koi pond. The boss agreed as long as Kenny and the construction crew built it and maintained it. The following spring, there stood a beautifully landscaped mini-waterfall that dropped into a rock-lined pool filled with fishes of various shades of orange and gold. He was so proud of the final result as were his coworkers and the seniors.

Often when he was sick and couldn't work, he'd wonder how his fishes were doing. Kenny's replacement at Brooksby would call and Kenny would talk him through the water purification and feeding instructions. No one could keep the water crystal clear and fish thriving like Kenny. This piece of paradise brought beauty and tranquility to an area once overrun by weeds and scrub brush.

Shortly after Kenny's passing, the Brooksby administration department contacted me. What they said gave me goose-bumps: In his absence, they had struggled to maintain the health of the koi pond, and during those few days while Kenny was at the hospice house, all of the fish died.

They had cleaned things up and got the koi pond going again, though, and planned a ceremony in June to dedicate the pond in Kenny's honor. I found this most touching because I knew how hard he had worked on it. Now the fruits of his labor would be commemorated. Family and close friends were invited.

My grief was still quite sharp, and I wasn't sure how I'd feel, going to the place where he had so loved his work, but I was so grateful at how much everyone there appreciated his contribution. Brooksby's executives and Kenny's coworkers greeted the two dozen of us who arrived. There was the pond with a wooden plaque in Kenny's name. The general manager spoke. Since Kenny's call number was seventeen, they had bought seventeen new fish to represent Kenny. It was a touching tribute. We gathered during refreshments, and reminisced. I was overcome by everyone's kind words.

Kenny's plaque at Brooksby Village

What helped me through my grief was knowing that I had no regrets. I had done everything I could for Kenny. I was always by his side and supported and loved him throughout all of his decisions. People would ask what was on our "bucket list," but we didn't have one. We always did what we wanted to do. Sometimes we did it "down the road," but we always did it. We vacationed with the kids, traveled together, and fulfilled most of our dreams. Too many folks leave it for tomorrow, but then tomorrow never comes and then it's too late. I came to realize that time does not heal: you just create a new way of living.

I was both happy and sad to go back to work in September. I needed that sense of purpose, but without Kenny, my heart was no longer into World of Wonder. The struggle to be there without him became unbearable. The time for me to leave World of Wonder and let someone else take up the reins was fast approaching.

A couple of months later, in November, I began to notice that Auntie was not quite right. She used to be sharp as a tack, planning activities and socializing with her friends. Now she was forgetful and confused. She was still driving, but when she got lost on her way to go shopping and hit a mailbox, I knew something was very wrong. After neurological testing, she was diagnosed with early-onset Alzheimer's disease and was put on Aricept. I couldn't believe how quickly things had changed for her. Poor Auntie and poor me!

I had been thinking about getting a puppy to keep me company. My two cats had become really weird and anti-social after Kenny died. They hid all the time, so I found another home for them. I researched hypoallergenic breeds that don't shed, and chose the mini-Goldendoodle cross-breed. A Massachusetts breeder in Sutton had puppies available, so off I went, with Eric, Monica, Drew, Jack and Emma in tow. We arrived at a rustic farmhouse to the sound of barking puppies. The breeder proudly displayed one adorable doodle after another. It was impossible to choose a favorite among them. Finally, she brought in an apricot-colored pup with his head snuggled on her shoulder. She mentioned that he had soulful eyes, and indeed, he did.

After we all played with him, there was no doubt he was meant to be mine. On that cold December day, we came home with my precious Jasper, formerly known as Duke. During snowstorms that winter I trained him and he became my best loyal buddy. He still is. It was great to come home and have him enthusiastically greet me. Even Auntie loved him. He would sit on the couch and watch game shows with her.

Jasper

Auntie insisted on returning to Treasure Island, in Florida, for the winter. I was apprehensive about this. I called her Florida friends to let them know about her condition, but they assured me that they would keep tabs on her. On the one hand, I needed a break from taking care of her. On the other hand, I knew I'd worry about her: Could she do her pills? Would she eat and drink enough?

We made a compromise, to escort her there ourselves and see her settled. Monica, Karen, and I flew down with her in January on Martin

Luther King, Jr., holiday weekend. On the way from the Tampa Airport to her condominium unit, she couldn't remember how to get to her favorite breakfast place. The condo was familiar to her—she had been going there for years. It was her home away from home; maybe she'd be okay, but she was still disoriented. Reluctantly we left on Monday and hoped for the best, after insisting that she was not to rent car while she was there.

She lasted about six weeks. Her friends called to report that her short-term memory had deteriorated so badly that she couldn't stay there any longer. They sent her home.

It was shocking to see how much she had declined in so short a time. Now she needed an at-home caregiver, so she would not be alone while I was at work. I interviewed the grandmother of one of our World of Wonder clients. She lived in Burlington and was looking for a part-time job. I hired her to take Auntie food shopping, to the hair salon, to Bingo, to breakfast, and to talk, laugh, and socialize with her.

It was such a help for me. As I had done for Kenny, I was now cooking meals for both of us, filling pill boxes, paying Auntie's bills, doing her laundry, doing her banking. I even picked out her clothes every day, otherwise Auntie would insist on wearing the same two outfits, clean or not.

I took her to primary-care appointments, neurologists, endocrinologists, physical therapists—you get the idea. Once a week she went to the Senior Center with her best friend and neighbor, Clair. They would play cards and Bingo. The social interaction was invaluable for her, and for me.

This went on for almost a year. Each month Auntie failed more and more. She became anxious when I was not with her and wouldn't ride in the car with anyone but me. She wanted to stay home all the time. Jasper spent most days with her and kept her company while she was alone. She deteriorated physically. She coughed a lot, her balance was off, and she was weak. Her blood pressure was now up, now down. Sometimes her stomach pained her. We had all sorts of people in and out of the house tending to her needs, but nothing helped. It was awful.

Auntie's caregiver called me at work one day to report that Auntie was not well. I rushed home and found her gagging and very lethargic. She had been aspirating into her lungs. I called an ambulance and she was admitted to Lahey Clinic in Burlington. They gave her IV fluids and tried to rehab her. She was confused—she didn't know where she was or who was caring for her. I met with her case manager, who recommended her admission into an assisted living facility. I knew that was coming, but I was still in denial. Kenny's loss was still too close to me. But I had to make an immediate decision.

Poor Auntie never came back to 6 Sheila Avenue. She was admitted into the Blair House in Tewksbury. I was heartbroken yet relieved. I couldn't care for her at home and keep her safe anymore, and it was too much even with an in-home nursing assistant.

I moved Auntie into her new apartment in Blair House. She stayed in assisted living for about two years. Then she fell and broke her nose. She was then moved into skilled care. That story is another entire book itself.

* * *

It hadn't been so long since I'd lost Kenny. I contemplated joining a bereavement group, but I was reluctant to talk about Kenny's death with complete strangers. The hospice house offered group sessions, but no way could I bear to enter that building again. Then I found a group in Winchester that was registering people for a six-week program at Saint Eulalia's Parish.

I always admired people who opened up enough to seek help for their issues. It was time I practiced what I preached. So, in the fall of 2015, off I went. One by one we filed in, six women and two men. Like an AA meeting, we shared our stories; some chose not to speak. There were lots of similarities and lots of differences in how we all happened to be there. I especially related to two women who chronicled their grief at losing their husbands. One woman, Claudette, sobbed as she described her wonderful marriage and life and how her loss was unbearable. I understood how she felt and we became fast friends. (We still are!) It was such a relief to talk to someone who really got it. We still talk to our mutual friend, Helen, who is inspirational to us. She has lost two husbands and tries to live every day to its fullest. We have all cried together but also laughed together. I am truly blessed to have them in my life.

In the first year after Kenny's death, people rallied around me, helping me and calling me to see how I was doing. By the second year, people figured that I was okay. That's typical; we need to move on with our own lives. But I was not okay. It was exhausting to pretend that I was all right. I was still an overwhelmed, scared, lonely widow.

After being alone for a while, I came to the conclusion that the world was created for couples. I learned I could be in a room full of people and still feel alone. Many years ago, when I'd see a group of single women together for a girls' night out, I never envied their freedom. Even at that young an age, I knew that I would rather be one of the couples toasting a glass of wine together. Instead of being half of a couple, however, now I sat in the widowed group. I never thought that this was how I would grow old.

* * *

As soon as people heard about Auntie's situation, they advised me to sell my house and move into a condominium unit, which would be more manageable. My kids and grandkids lived in Tewksbury and liked it. It was hard to talk about selling the house that Kenny and I had built and loved, but downsizing was a practical and reasonable option.

Monica's friend, Seana, who dealt in real estate, found a young couple that was interested in my property. I was reluctant, but decided to let them walk through. The woman's father had passed away recently and her mother wanted to move with them. The house with Auntie's in-law apartment downstairs was ideal. They loved it and wanted to give me an offer that night, but I put them off until after the weekend. If I agreed to sell, I had better find a place to live.

On Friday, Monica, Seana, and I spent the day at open houses and private showings. We found nothing that suited me. Close to noon on Saturday, however, we viewed a corner-unit townhouse at Patten Green Condos in Tewksbury. It was newly renovated with a modern twist that suited my style. It was bright and cheery with great natural lighting. We all loved it. For the first time ever, I could actually imagine living somewhere else. I put an offer in and within a few hours, my offer was accepted. Then I accepted the full bid offer for my place from the couple with the mother.

This brief description makes it sound easy, but making these monumental decisions alone without Kenny's guidance consumed me. It was another of my inevitable steps "down the road" without my beloved Kenny.

Visiting Auntie at Blair House

CHAPTER FIVE

Quail

- - - - - - - - - - - - - - - - - -

Downsizing my thirty-two-hundred square-foot house, in which I had lived in for thirty-eight years, was the next challenge. Three garages, two sheds, and Auntie's apartment needed to be emptied. Eric rented a dumpster for me, so huge that I could walk into it. When the company hauled it out of there a month later, it was filled to capacity, covered with a tarp to keep things from flying out the top during transport.

After truckloads of trips from Woburn to Tewksbury and tons of help from family and friends, I moved into my new townhouse, in early September at 5 Quail Run in Tewksbury. The months of emotional and physical upheaval all summer certainly took its toll on me. Initially I felt like I was on vacation, but by and by, the place became familiar and I came to enjoy living there. It was a fresh start for me, exactly what I needed.

As if my life wasn't hectic enough, at the end of June 2016, in the middle of this whole downsizing and moving mess, I met a nice man. I had never dated—Kenny and I had been true to each other since our teens—so this was a brand-new experience. Our connection was instant, and we dated for three years, traveling together and enjoying each other's company. We finally parted because our lives were headed in different directions. This relationship taught me that I could be happy again and care for someone else, so I have no regrets. He just wasn't the man for me.

Over the next few years, I got together with Kenny's cousin Paul regularly. We reminisced about all the crazy stuff he and Kenny did when they were kids. Paul contracted Parkinson's disease and was not doing well. His balance was off and his body was stiff and rigid. I'm so glad we got together in those last years because before we knew it, Paul was gone, too.

His passing was sudden. It was sad to lose him at such a relatively young age. Losing him, too, made it hard to cope, and I still miss him deeply. My only comfort was knowing that he and Kenny are together again. Paul's dad, Uncle Paul, is a kind and gentle man who loves to garden and do wood-working. I have a great relationship with him and his daughter Dianne. My sisters-in-law, Paula and Marsha, keep in touch with them, too.

Paula, Dianne, Uncle Paul & Marsha

Shortly after, our Rennell family dynamics underwent major changes. Monica and Jay had been having marital problems for a while. They had grown apart. They had tried to work things out without success. They had married young, and Emma and Cameron had come along shortly after. This was a turbulent time for them and all of us who loved them. At the end of the summer, Monica met with an attorney and asked Jay for a divorce. Needless to say, everyone was sad about this.

It was an adjustment for everyone, especially the kids. Joint custody was a new concept to me, half the week with Mom and half the week with

Dad. Since then, Monica and Jay have worked successfully to restore an amicable relationship for the sake of Emma and Cam. They are both good parents. I am proud that they made sure their kids are their top priority. We're friendly enough to sit together at the kids' activities, and Jay will always be dear to my heart.

I was still commuting from Tewksbury to WOW in Woburn. Having owned and run the preschool for thirty years, I was ready to retire. Monica had worked there for several years, so she took it over in May 2017. I was so happy to keep our business in the family, and relieved that I no longer had the liability and responsibility.

When I left, so did Joan, Terry, Denise, Mary, and Linda C. Following our final graduation, I had a luncheon with them and we exchanged gifts and lots of great memories. The girls continue to get together a few times a year, to keep in touch. We call them The Fab Five. Occasionally Monica calls me to help out, and I am happy to sit in my old office, like a fish out of water having jumped back into the tank.

The Fab Five & me (from left):
Linda C., Terry, me, Denise, Joan, & Mary

To celebrate my retirement, the kids surprised me with a party. They designed a Hawaiian theme and rented a photo booth, of all things. It was a great time with my family, staff and friends. As usual, life is bittersweet. I enjoyed the gathering greatly, but I missed Kenny. I always will.

These days I hang out with Jasper, go to local music concerts and the movies, and eat out way too much. When I remember the endless hours I spent in the kitchen, cooking and cleaning, I marvel at how, today, I don't feel driven to do that anymore. It is lousy to cook and eat alone all the time. Watching TV alone stinks, too. My pal Jasper, always by my side, makes me laugh away the loneliness.

I love attending my grandkids' extracurricular activities. I try to go to every baseball, basketball, soccer, flag football, lacrosse, hockey, and track event. It gives me such pleasure to be a part of their lives and watch them grow into wonderful young men and women. Kenny's genes are apparent in some of them, especially Drew and Emma physical features. I see them all happy and healthy, and I know Kenny lives on through them. I know he is proud of the adults Eric and Monica that have become. They are both successful and kind. Eric now owns his own company, Rennell Capital Group, a construction consultant business. Karen is the director of MIT's construction company. Monica successfully runs World of Wonder. Drew, Jack, Emma, Cameron and Molly—three teenagers and two tweens—are growing up much too quickly. They are all doing well in school and have lots of friends. I couldn't ask for more.

CHAPTER SIX

Kendall

- - - - - - - - - - - - - - - -

We have reached the final chapter. I thought it would be fitting for my children and grandchildren to complete my memoir. When I asked them, they all had questions and concerns about what to write. Their assignment was simply to write about Kenny. There was no format or requirements. I knew they would all do great and they have not disappointed. Their interpretations are unique to their individual relationships with him. These are their unedited writings.

ERIC

My Dad

nature, protector, fisherman, wonderful, heart of gold,
could fix anything, tinkerer, snowmobiles, happy, bird lover,
animal lover, loved his yard, projects, tools, garages,
lending a helping hand, down to earth, organized/semi hoarder,
supportive, go-kart, 905 Main Street, never give up, classic cars,
drop anything to help, Eagles Band, Tahoe, model building,
karate, Friendly's strawberry Fribble,
short ripped jean shorts, radio/stereo blasting, make breakfast,
drive-thrus, Brooksby Village, Polaroid, World of Wonder,
pine trees, cancer, Leon, Paul, family, Papa,
simple, proud, Linda,
55 Chevy, 31 Hot Rod, 78 Trans Am, 70 Duster, 32 Hudson

MONICA

When I think about my Dad and what he meant to me, several things come to mind:

Committed - Growing up, I can remember how he treated my mother and us. He always put us first and made sure we were taken care of, emotionally and financially. He would always check in to see how my day was and let us know when he was home from work. If I needed anything, he was readily available and gave me anything a little girl could want. Even as I became an adult, he was still there for me and my children. Every winter he always reminded me to have an ice scraper, a small shovel, and a can of defroster in my car.

Vacations - He worked hard all year so we could go on at least one vacation a year. I have so many fond memories of the four of us driving or flying to different destinations. We visited Florida, North and South Carolinas, Georgia, DC, Virginia, and Bermuda, to name a few. We had many fights and laughs during these travels, and he always said to stop whining and check the view out the window.

Determination - He made all of my mother's dreams come true by building her a school and a house that we all loved. We used to call it Rennell Resort. He had a fine work ethic and never was a quitter. I remember my parents doing endless projects at their business and house. Later when I had my own home, he advised us about improvements and always had great ideas.

Quick temper - My Dad was calm and easy-going until someone crossed the line with him or one of us. He taught me how to stick up for myself and not to let anyone give me grief. When someone wrongly questioned him, then he lost it. The most important lesson was if you are wrong, own up to it and take responsibility for your actions.

Papa - He was so thrilled that we were having a girl since my brother had twin boys. When he found out about Emma in 2006, he was happy to have his first granddaughter. He treated her like a princess and never missed any of her milestones. Less than two years later my parents brought me to my first ultrasound where he found out about his third grandson, Cameron, arriving in seven months. They were very joyful years that we all shared together.

I carry these memories with me today as an adult and a mother. I commit myself to everything I do in my life, whether it is with my family or career. My kids always come first, which I learned from my Dad at a young age. I feel like I am determined and always find a way to get things done. I especially have inherited my Dad's temper which helps me to be a productive member of society.

Thanks Dad!

KAREN

Papa's Song
My Father-in-Law, Kenny

"Cause you'll be in my heart. Yes, you'll be in my heart. From this day on. Now and Forever more…Always…Just look over your shoulder…Just look over your shoulder…I'll be there…Always." (Phil Collins)

Shortly after my father-in-law, Kenny, passed away, my four-year-old and I were listening to Disney Radio. "You'll Be in My Heart" by Phil Collins came on. As Molly and I twirled around our living room, my little girl turned to me and simply said, "Papa's Song." She was spot-on. The words in this song are the epitome of the empathy and legacy of Kenny Rennell; "Just look over your shoulder…I'll be there…Always."

When Eric and I had the twins, we outgrew our townhouse the day we brought them home. We moved to a family-friendly neighborhood into a home with all the space and yard we dreamed of, but there was lots of work to be done. We were a young couple so the majority of the work was self-performed, on our own time. Kenny showed up for every project with all the tools, gadgets, supplies, good humor, and smiles we would need. Sometimes my phone would ring and Kenny would be on the other line. He would brainstorm ideas with me. He was my partner in crime convincing Eric about which one of my many ideas should be our next project. "Just look over your shoulder…I'll be there…Always."

Our house is full of Kenny: the paint, the woodwork, tree house, hallway doors, the birch tree (Kenny's favorite), the porch, the deck, the kitchen door, the pine trees, the bird feeders, the shelves, picture frames, the wind chimes, the mailbox … The list is endless. "Just look over your shoulder…I'll be there…Always."

Five years after Kenny passed, Eric and I were now very established in our careers. We had maximized every nook and cranny of our home with our three children. Many families would look for a larger home, but this house was our labor of love and a perfect fit in our eyes. We decided to pursue a new dream of buying a small beach house 45 minutes north on the Maine Coast. We knew Kenny would love this idea if he were here and be so proud of us. We pulled up to a small ranch on Angel Ave in York. Angel Avenue … hmmm … The house was small but cozy in a great location and it had a garage which we needed for additional space to store Kenny's 55 Chevy that Eric now proudly owned. There was lots of potential for projects, of course, but this little house was perfect for us and reminded us of our home in Massachusetts. As we walked around, I saw signs.

This house was full of Kenny: The street name—Angel Avenue—two thriving birch trees in the front yard, the large garage, the deck, the spacious yard. The most significant sign was found tucked away in a small linen closet. I looked at Eric with surprise and exclaimed, "There's a laundry chute!" This was the second laundry chute I had ever seen in my life—the first was in Eric's childhood home, where Kenny had built one discreetly tucked under a bathroom cabinet. "Just look over your shoulder…I'll be there…Always."

As the years move along, Kenny is everywhere: at soccer games, family parties, completing house projects with our three children, and beach trips. "Just look over your shoulder…I'll be there…Always."

DREW

Everyone says that I look like my Papa ... He must have been a pretty good-looking kid. I'm named after him, my middle name, which is Kenneth. I had awesome memories with my Papa. When my mom and dad had to go to work early, Jack, Molly, and I would get dropped off at my Nonna and Papa's house for the day. One thing we did when we were there was study the giant map my Papa brought home. He would explain whatever questions we had about what was happening in the world.

Another memory I have is going to the New England Dragway in Epping, New Hampshire. Jack, my dad, and Papa would sit for hours watching all of the cars do burnouts and wheelies and fly down the track. We all love cars, this is one true passion we all shared. I would always be excited to go for a ride in the 1955 Chevy 210 he had and the 1968 Chevy Camaro my dad had at the time. We would attend car shows on the weekend whenever we could. I loved helping Papa with the hot rod he wanted to finish or working on the go-kart he bought for us. When we drove the go-kart, he would grab his blue yard chair and two cones and sit in the middle of the road watching out for us.

My Papa also taught me valuable lessons and tips that made things a lot easier. Such as labeling and organizing parts or switches or how to do certain things when we were fishing.

He left a lesson of a lifetime … to never give up. No matter what challenge you face, whether or not you think you can keep going … to never give up.

My family and I watch old tape recordings and in a few of them my Papa is there. He may sound a little different than I remember. He may look a little different than I remember. But I will never forget the impact he had on my life and the people around him. Every once and awhile my dad will say, "Papa taught me this" or "Papa showed me that." It truly reminds me of how great an effect he had on everyone's lives.

Because of these lessons and the tips he taught me, it makes me who I am today. I am proud to carry on his name and his ways. I am going to tell my family's future generations about him and keep his memory alive.

JACK

When my Papa was diagnosed with cancer, I was only four years old. At the time I did not understand the seriousness of his illness. Part of the reason being that he never showed signs of weakness when we were around him. He was a fighter and he was tough, he was also a great grandfather who was caring and fun. My Papa always tried to get my brother Drew and me to learn something new or teach us a lesson that would stick with us forever. My Papa was a role model to me and he still is to this day. I am fourteen years old now and not a day goes by where I don't use a life skill that he taught me. My grandfather also taught me to be the best version of myself. No matter what, he always tried to make other people happy. And that made him happy, too. I share that trait with him and he helped shape who I am today.

A lot of my favorite things to do I used to do with him and my Dad. The biggest thing I get from him is my interests in cars. He had a 1955 Chevrolet 210 Coupe—he would take us for rides in it all of the time when we were over his house. My Dad owns that car now and in two years I will get the chance to drive it just like my Papa and my Dad did. Every time I see it, I think of him and all of the unforgettable memories we had with his car.

There is one tradition that we first started with my Papa that my brother, my Dad, and I observe every year. Every year we would have a boys' fishing trip with other people in my large family. We would go up to Jackman, Maine, where we would stay on an island for three days in the middle of a lake and go out on boats and fish all day. We stayed in log cabins; in mine was my Dad, my brother, and my grandfather. While we were fishing all four of us were squished together on a small aluminum boat. It was in this small little boat and in the log cabin where I have some of the best memories of my grandfather. To this day every year we still stay in the same cabin. I still use the same tips and tricks he taught me. And I still catch more fish than he did. My Dad recently found some old videos of a fishing trip we all took. I remember it like it was yesterday and I still miss him.

Eventually my Papa's battle with his illness was too overwhelming to hide it any longer from us. At this point he had been fighting it for years. Although we could see he was physically tired and exhausted, his mindset still stayed the same. Throughout his entire battle with cancer, he was always the same loving, funny, caring, kind-hearted person who would do anything for us. He was one of the greatest examples of a true man. I want to grow up to be like him. I want to help people, make people happy, make them smile, have a good time, enjoy life, and be the best man I can be.

Just like my Papa.

EMMA

My love for my Papa

For the five-year anniversary of my Papa's death, our family got together at my aunt and uncle's house to show pictures, watch videos, and share wonderful memories of Papa. It was both happy and sad since he is no longer with us. But we were lucky to have him for as long as we did and he struggled through years of chemotherapy to stay with my Nonna and us as long as he could. He got stage-four bowel cancer at a young age. One thing I loved most about Papa was we got to go to the timeshare at Sea Mist in Cape Code. Every third week in July, my Nonna and Papa took my Mom and Uncle there, ever since they were young. I had never skipped a year. I will never forget how excited I was to swim in the resort's indoor pool even though they wouldn't let me. This is where he taught me how to dive just like he did with my Mom when she was young. I was so nervous but he told me to duck down low and put my hands up over my head. He was right there with me, in the pool to guide my dive. He gave me confidence and believed in me and so I trusted him and I did it. Every year when I'm in that same spot in the pool, I think of him. He would take us for walks and little hikes through the woods and all of us would get breakfast at Dunkin Donuts. Later in the day we would walk to the store to get candy for us. He never sat around, he was always adventurous and up for trying something new.

Another memory is riding in his Chevy. He would beep his loud horn and wave and people would give us a thumbs-up. Not many people have a classic car like his so it was special to ride around with him, my brother, and my Nonna to go get ice cream. We thought we were so cool! Nonna and Papa's house in Woburn was beautiful inside and outside and there was so much to do there. They had an outdoor and an inside hot tub. They were large so we could all go in and swim a little on and under the water. The indoor room had a TV set up so we could hang and watch our favorite shows. The outside one had cold water and was like a mine pool with jets and a geyser in the middle. This was something my Nonna always wanted and boy! did we all enjoy them, winter and summer. Overall, I think of my Papa as a brave, strong and helpful person. When he got cancer, I was only three years old, but I am thankful that he lived four more years so we had time to make memories with him that I still can remember. I know my Nonna misses him a lot and I wish he was still here today. His body could not fight the disease anymore, but I admire him for fighting to stay alive so he could spend more time with all of us.

I miss and love you so much, Papa!

CAMERON

I love my Papa and miss him so much and I know my Nonna misses him even more. They loved to do fun things together or just sit and have tea and talk. I was only one year old when he got sick, so I only remember some stuff. He got a go-kart for me, my sister, and cousins. We would drive it on Sheila Avenue which was a dead-end street. We always had to wear our helmets that he bought us and he would let us drive it fast. It was so much fun! Also, when he was too sick to work, my Mom and Nonna went to work at World of Wonder and he would babysit me and Molly. We would have an intense game of checkers, and one day after I lost, I flung the board across the room 'cuz I don't like to lose. He got mad but later we laughed about it, but even though I was just a kid, he was not going to let me win unless I earned it. He always made me try hard and work for things, which was a good lesson to learn even though I did not think so at the time.

I really wish he was still here to watch me play hockey, baseball, basketball, and flag football. I know he would be proud of me since I tried my best and he would be there cheering me on. I would also like to mention something that my Mom and I do all the time and we have made it Our Thing since he died. Whenever we tell each other something and may doubt each other, we say, "Do you swear on Papa?" We do that because we know he is watching us. When I grow up, I will make sure to let my kids keep some of the family traditions that we did when my Papa was alive!

What the words Papa and Kenny represent:

P = Positive A = Active P = Playful A = Amazing
K = Kind E = Energetic N = Neat N = Nurturing Y = Youthful

MOLLY

The one thing I will always remember about my Papa was how kind and loving he was. When he passed away, I was only five years old, but even though I was young I still remember him. My favorite memory of him is when my cousin Cam and I were riding in the front seat because Papa had all his tools in the back. Since we were both young at the time we were supposed to be in the back seat. There was a cop car down the street and he would tell us both to duck down. Cam and I would drop to the floor as we were all giggling so we would not get caught. When the coast was clear, we popped up and kept our eyes open for another cruiser. Thankfully we did not see another one. Most times when I went to their house, we would usually find Papa in one of his many garages working on one of his cars. He loved them all. I still think of him almost every day. I will always love him. I am happy that he was my grandfather. I know he is in Heaven watching down on me and is proud of my school grades and my sport accomplishments and that I am a good person like he was.

FINALE

After my mother died in February of 2015, I reconciled with my brother, Johnny, for which I'm very grateful. Now my family gets together with his wife, Tracy, and their daughter, Jordan. I also have two nieces from his first marriage, Michelle and Melissa.

Monica is now married to Shawn and they are very happy together. He is a firefighter and paramedic and is a wonderful guy. He has a son named Hunter and is so good to Emma and Cameron. They have successfully blended their families and I have gained a new step-grandson. They own a beautiful home in Tewksbury and are starting their new life together.

Monica & her husband Shawn

**My grandchildren, Cam & Emma,
and my new step-grandson, Hunter**

My children and grandchildren are finding their own roads to follow. There is the void of not having their father and grandfather in their lives. We all knew when Kenny said, "Down the road," at this point in his life he meant when he was no longer with us. He was always mindful to prepare us for life without him. Now that he is gone, I reflect on all the little jobs he taught us. At that time, we did not want to hear those words but we are grateful to him now for guiding us.

ON TO A NEW ADVENTURE ON DEBRA DRIVE!
STAY TUNED!

CONCLUSION

I was angry with God for allowing such a good-hearted and family-oriented guy like Kenny to suffer and die the way he did. I used to tell my priest friend, Father Lynch, that I did not want to pray anymore. He said to let other people pray for us. Those were good words of advice. He was a great man who always led me in the right direction. He was a wonderful mentor to both Kenny and me.

The phrase "moving on" is a complicated one. I have agonized for several years as to what it means to me. I still yearn for the life I once had, and my loss is still draining after all these years. I now realize that feeling either guilty or disrespectful is useless. I am a work-in-progress and trying to live my life with gratitude, trying to find happiness along the way. Self-improvement is a life journey. The power of true love can never be underestimated, and once you find it, there is no better gift. Building a fulfilling life with someone, founded on trust and mutual respect, is truly amazing and incredible. If you gain material things along the way, that's a bonus, but the core relationship is what makes a couple rich. So, live your life. Do not wait until life throws you a curve ball and cuts off your time.

Our 36th Wedding Anniversary

I am self-sufficient, independent, healthy, and blessed by many people who genuinely love me. A part of me, however, died on that Friday night at Kaplan House. I still miss telling Kenny about the bad and good things that happen. He always fixed things for all of us and I still often feel like I am floundering. I don't feel whole anymore. Throughout the years, we were blessed with such a wonderful network of family and friends. We truly could not have survived this horrible experience without each and every one of them. I am forever grateful for all their love and support. I still have a great life. Except for a little arthritis and sore knees, I am always busy. I intend to continue to live what is left of my life trying to be a good person.

I will never be complete until I am reunited with Kenny again. I keep my heart open because that is what he wanted me to do. But since that dreadful May night, I have never felt as secure as I always did when he was by my side.

My life has never been the same without him. "Linda without Kenny" can never experience the pure joy and endless love that "Linda and Kenny" shared. Some people are never lucky enough to find true love in their life. I was fortunate to have it, but the burden of living without it does not lessen the pain.

If you are blessed enough to have that someone special, never take advantage of him or her. Always respect each other and show them every day that they are your top priority. Communicate with each other, be considerate of their feelings, support their dreams, love deeply and passionately. Pray that your soulmate does not get taken away from you by an accident or illness. Spend your days making each other happy. Live every day like it's your last. It could be.

Auntie Lorraine was the matriarch of my family and Uncle Paul is the patriarch of Kenny's family. Their years of combined experience in relationships benefited all of us without measure.

Auntie always said, "Never go to bed mad." Whenever any of us argued with our significant others, she urged us to straighten things out before we fell asleep. God forbid: if something happened through the night, one would never forgive themselves. Before Auntie got Alzheimer's, she was a nervous worrywart. Sometimes with this disease it exacerbates one's temperament, but it proved the opposite with her: she became relaxed and indifferent. Thereafter when anything good or bad happened, she smiled and said, "It is what it is." So true!

Uncle Paul says that to have a good marriage, you should always think, "We, not just me." His simple words of wisdom go a long way!

Unfortunately, Auntie passed away in July 2021 and I have stepped into her role. It's very weird for me to be the oldest female in our family, the new matriarch. She endowed us with happy memories and sage advice. She was always a positive role model to me and her legacy lives on in me, my children, and my grandchildren.

ACKNOWLEDGEMENTS

Every author has others to credit for a book's completion. I too have people to thank for assisting me.

Allison Tarin is a friend and the office manager at World of Wonder. About two years ago, I presented her with my handwritten journal-like jumble of pages, the nucleus of this story. She brilliantly organized these words into readable chapters. She made several changes and typed a rough draft. She was always just a phone call away and I made many trips to her office for copies. Then the manuscript was ready for a publisher.

A special thanks goes to my family and friends who supported my endeavor. Their encouragement gave me the confidence to keep writing. They helped me to recap vital facts and inspired me to continue writing this, my first book. A special shout out to my daughter-in-law, Karen, for the chapter names. She helped me to make them meaningful and symbolic. Eric and Monica's proofreading improved my spelling and punctuation, and I thank my twin grandson, Drew, for his organizational skills and grammar edits. His brother, Jack, designed the symbolic book cover.

Thanks to my readers who choose to embark on paths similar to mine. As Kenny and I chose them, consciously or otherwise, they each took us a little farther "down the road."

Printed in the United States
by Baker & Taylor Publisher Services